PRESENTED TO

_____

FROM

_____

DATE

_____

HOUSE RULES

HOUSE RULES

HOW TO DECORATE FOR EVERY HOME, STYLE, AND BUDGET

MYQUILLYN SMITH

Revell
a division of Baker Publishing Group
Grand Rapids, Michigan

CONTENTS

Introduction   7

RULES 1–35
DO WHAT YOU KNOW

RULES 36–66
USE WHAT YOU HAVE

RULES 67–100
FINISH WHAT YOU STARTED

100 House Rules   233

Acknowledgments   235

Notes   237

INTRODUCTION

I CAME CLOSE to flunking spelling every year of grade school. I dreaded Fridays because it meant there was a spelling test, and I wasn't good at spelling. I'm still not. The problem was, I believed the purpose of the test was to find out what I already knew, not to help encourage me to learn. I didn't realize we were allowed, much less expected, to study the spelling words. Wasn't that cheating? You either knew how to spell the words or you didn't. I didn't.

Now that I'm a grown-up I know that spelling is a skill I can learn. No one is born knowing how to spell. There is no spelling gene. It's the same with decorating. No one is born with the decorating gene. Decorating is simply making informed decisions in the right order. Like any skill, you get better with practice.

I can teach you how to make better decorating decisions with confidence.

It's one thing to see a pretty photo of a room and know you like how it looks. It's a completely different thing to look up at your own room and wonder why, even though you've chosen every item in there, you don't love it. Where do you begin? How do you know what changes to focus on and what not to worry about?

When you get a new appliance you can turn to the back of the manual where there's a troubleshooting area. It explains that if the light won't stop blinking, it's probably not broken and could be caused by one of four things. Think of *House Rules* as your manual for home; these rules and tips guide you in how to troubleshoot. Don't like your family room? That's actually more common than you might think. Let's walk through some universal decorating truths and see what you're missing.

Decorating is a skill you can learn.

People often think that the skill is picking out a room full of stylish items that function great and look beautiful together without making any mistakes. The secret is, the actual skill is understanding what to do when a roomful of stuff DOESN'T look good together. Now what? That's where this book meets you. I want to help you figure out what to do when you're in a real room in a real house that isn't perfect—when you can't buy all new stuff and you're faced with a bunch of decisions. That's what I love to do.

I have a method for approaching big projects that begins with three mantras I repeat to myself so I won't get overwhelmed. These mantras have helped me in my business, in my home, and in my everyday life, and this book is organized by working through these steps:

Do what you know.
Use what you have.
Finish what you started.

While different versions of these mantras have been said by lots of folks, this book is my take on three universal truths that can help you through an astonishing array of circumstances.

Unlike other home books written by designers with lots of finished client homes to photograph, this book features only one home: mine. This is our classroom, my laboratory. It's my job to keep the photos interesting, fresh, and inspiring. And I'm up for the challenge! You might notice the same chair, accessory, or doohickey in different rooms, and this is exactly how I live—moving things around based on the season and which of our boys is currently living at home and the most recent secondhand find I'm obsessed with.

This is not a style book. I don't expect you to love my style; I expect you to love *your* style. I expect you to want to learn from me because I know how to make confident decorating decisions that transcend personal style.

I love my house, and I promise you can love yours too. ■

DO
WHAT
YOU
KNOW

WE WERE FIVE YEARS into living in a fixer-upper, and it was time to tackle the upstairs. There were just two bedrooms, a thirty-six-inch-wide hallway, and a tiny bathroom. Except I was tired and overwhelmed and didn't know where to begin. Every single thing needed attention. So I decided to take three mantras I had used in my business and apply them to my house: do what I know, use what I have, and finish what I started.

What did I know? At first it felt like nothing. But I looked around. We had no heating or air-conditioning upstairs and had been using window units and space heaters for years. When we moved in we had pulled up stained carpet and painted the subfloor but hadn't touched it since. I might not have had a big design plan, but I knew I had to begin with the basics. I knew a house had to have heat and air and actual floors. We got a new HVAC unit and decided to install real flooring.

To make the house cohesive and make my decisions easier, I again decided to do what I knew by piggybacking off decisions I was already happy with on the first floor. I repeated materials I loved as we updated the flooring, ceiling, trim, and paint colors. Because I chose to move forward by starting with doing what I actually knew to do, we made progress and I felt confident in my decisions. Instead of the decisions exhausting me, they energized me. I earned some momentum to keep going.

I know what it feels like to face a literal houseful of decisions and suddenly feel tired, overwhelmed, and like you need to eat a donut. I have a long history of making things more difficult than they need to be and assuming I need to know everything before I can even begin to make a difference.

Decorating starts *in your head*, not the furniture store. Your thinking, goals, and priorities need to be right before you start picking paint colors or buying a sofa. That's the first step to any big project—simply start with what you need to know. Sometimes you already know a lot, sometimes you have to do a bit of research, and sometimes you simply need to refresh your memory.

This first section is full of basic truths and house rules to jump-start your thinking. They are simple and memorable so you can repeat them to yourself, your friends, and the cashier at Target. Here's what I know when it comes to making changes in your home . . .

1

Learn the rules to break the rules

WELCOME TO AN ENTIRE BOOK full of rules to decorate by written by a person who doesn't care for rules all that much! Rules are great when it comes to understanding which side of the street to drive on, standing in line at a theme park, and cooking the perfect poached egg. Rules aren't so great when applied to creative endeavors.

When it comes to art forms, one purpose of rules is to provide a general framework for order. An artist can bend or break these rules from time to time in a way that makes the art better than it would have been otherwise.

You are the artist and your home is your canvas. It's imperative that you understand the rules of decorating so that when you choose to break one, it's on purpose and not because you have no idea about the fundamentals of good design. Break the rules so things can be better, not because you don't know better.

Often the most memorable part of any art form is the unexpected. The musician changes the key of the chorus. The architect adds a modern addition to a historical home. The Etsy seller adds a bubblegum bubble to a Mona Lisa print.

Read, learn, and apply these rules. Then go forth and break them beautifully and with purpose. Your home will be better for it. ▪

2

Find a mindset you can model

SOMETIMES I'LL SHARE a photo of my house on social media and someone will leave a comment telling me how much they dislike my style and the room and that I did it all wrong and it's ugly. There's always a part of me that wants to comment back and let them know I'm open to their opinion on personal style, but first I'll need to see some pictures of their rooms so I know if I can trust their judgment. If someone with rooms that aren't my style thinks my room is ugly, well, maybe that's exactly how it should be.

I'm not hoping to get anyone to love my style. We all have different styles after all. If you want to find people to take advice from, it's helpful to look for people doing the thing you want to do *in the way you want to do it*. Notice I didn't say to look for people doing the thing you want to do in THE EXACT WAY you want to do it. This isn't about finding a style

mentor you can mimic or copy (although from time to time that might be needed). This is about a mindset you can model.

I'll pay attention and learn from people who are making different decisions in their home if we have the same kinds of goals, even if their home isn't my style. Someone who wants a beautiful, functional, quirky, imperfect, welcoming, creative, soulful home is exactly who I want to learn from, regardless of whether I like their coffee table. There's a difference between someone making good decorating decisions and someone whose unique style is similar to my own. Please know this.

In business, I can learn helpful principles from someone even if their business has nothing to do with mine. But if I don't like the way a person runs their business, I don't care what they have to say even if we are in the same industry. It's important to decide who to ignore.

This is why when someone offers an unsolicited opinion about something in my house—especially when it's an opinion about my unique style—I always first consider the source, and so should you. ▪

Limitations lead to innovations

HENRI MATISSE IS QUOTED as saying, "Much of the beauty that arises in art comes from the struggle an artist wages with his limited medium." This quote gives me so much hope as a person whose home and circumstances are always up against some type of limits: time, money, control. Limitations are the entire point; they are the key to good ideas, creativity, beauty, art. Instead of hating them, we should welcome them. This is why I often refer to them as lovely limitations.

When we moved to our current home, the previous owners had left a pair of gorgeous custom-made drapes in the dining room. They were made from a shimmery fabric with a heavy felt liner, hemmed to custom perfection, and tailored for the windows as if the King of England himself would inspect them. Poor me, right? There was only one problem. The color. Although I'm a fan of a muddy blue, these drapes were icy. I'm a warm-color girl when it comes to our home interior, and these drapes bossed the entire room and brought the visual temperature down a few degrees. When it comes to decorating, I've learned I need **to respect my boss** (see house rule #20), but the shiny fab-

ric brought in a sense of formality that isn't quite on-brand with our family's casualness.

I've never had gorgeous custom drapes, so I challenged myself to try to make them work. I decided to welcome the limits and see if I could somehow offset the cold and proper presence of the drapes. I needed to neutralize and casualize.

I had a few strands of a warm, rustic, off-white garland with oversized cotton tassels that I had used on our fireplace the Christmas before, and I wondered if their primitive, earthy feel would help warm up and balance out the drapes. I grabbed the stepladder, pinned up a garland, and instantly knew this was going to work. The cozy oversized garland was the perfect mismatched complement to the drapes, **combining opposites** (#62) in a way that brought the drapes down a notch to our level of whimsy and approachability. The tassel garland is borderline ridiculous in size, and that's one of the reasons it's a perfect companion for the overly formal regal drapes. It helps the drapes not take themselves too seriously.

I'm so glad I didn't give up on those drapes even though I thought I could never make them work. It turns out that giving myself time to let ideas percolate and trying something halfway absurd was the key to a creative solution that is now one of my favorite combinations.

Got limitations? Consider them lovely and consider yourself lucky. ◼

Home exists to serve people, not the other way around

DO YOU KNOW how to tell when a home is in a good place? When it serves the people who live there and interacts with them seamlessly. When there's not a bunch of fretting over stuff, when there isn't angst about the home, and when the home partners with its inhabitants to be the place where they live their good life.

As you make decisions in your home, ask yourself, Does this solution help my home serve me better, or does it make me a servant to my home?

Our family room needed some extra seating and there was room in front of the fireplace/TV combo for a pair of chairs. Swivel chairs seemed like a great, functional option. The fireplace wall where I needed them was dark, and I knew if I wanted to actually see the chairs they should be a lighter color because **contrast is queen if you want to be seen** (#64).

The only problem was that, unlike light-colored furniture of my past, these chairs didn't have slipcovers I could wash when they got dirty. I knew from experience that the arms of the chairs would get the most wear and tear. So rather than working for my house, standing guard over my chairs and warning people to be careful with them and not wipe their filthy grimy hands on the precious arms, I simply added arm covers that worked for us. Instead of the grandma arm covers of my youth made from leftover chair fabric, I bought four light-colored rabbit pelts for $10 each, one for each arm.

Now I don't give our light-colored chairs a second thought. They are there to do their job and hold hineys, spinning us from TV-watching to conversation-having. They serve us without me being overly protective of them. My house works for me. Your house should work for you too. ▪

Resourcefulness is the ultimate resource

MOTIVATIONAL SPEAKER Tony Robbins is always saying that the ultimate resource is resourcefulness. It's just about the most profound thing I've ever heard.

In our twenty-nine years of marriage, Chad and I have lived in fifteen homes. We've lived in rentals with lots of restrictions, townhomes, tiny homes, a Civil War-era mansion that might have been haunted, builder-grade homes, country homes, and city homes.

When we had no money to spend on our house, I was sure that having a bigger budget was the solution.

When we were raising three tiny boys and had no margin, I knew that if I only had the time I could get our house looking the way I wanted.

When we lived in rentals with a list of things we couldn't change, I cursed the landlord under my breath and believed that freedom to paint the walls was the answer to my house woes.

When I finally had time, a little budget, and the freedom to make changes, I realized that there was something I was lacking: creativity. I was tired and had no inspiration or motivation.

I used to think I needed all of everything—money, time, control, inspiration, and motivation—to make meaningful changes in our home. But I can tell you from too much experience that you only need a little of some of those to start creating a home you love. When it comes to creating home, **there are other ways to pay** (#31).

Your willingness to begin without perfect circumstances is your most valuable resource. Right now is the time to create the home you've always wanted, starting with the stuff you already have. ■

6

Baby-step your way

ONE OF THE FIRST PIECES of furniture I can remember painting was our old dining room set. A huge black hutch, a large oval black table with two leaves, and eight black chairs were no match for me and this new stuff called chalk paint. By the time I was done with the hutch and table, I had convinced myself I could work with the black chairs because the thought of painting even one chair made me want to cut off my hands. Also, for some reason I started this project when our friend Scott was in town, so not only did I pick the largest pieces of furniture we had, but I started with an audience. The naivety. The nerve. The boldness. The fool.

When you are learning something about decorating and want to implement it, please do the exact opposite of what I did. Start with the smallest, least risky, least public thing you can and see what happens. Want to paint a piece of furniture? Wonderful. Go to the garage and grab that eight-dollar side table you bought last year from a yard sale and don't even like. Start with that because

you can't ruin something you already hate (#7). If it turns out awful, just drop it off at a thrift store. Nobody has to know.

When we start large and publicly, the pressure is on. There's no room for error, learning, or quietly moving on.

The third piece of furniture Chad and I purchased together was a custom sofa. We were so lucky, right? Yes, but sadly we were so dumb! I had never purchased an upholstered piece before. I really should have started with an off-the-rack chair so I could learn about scale and fabrics and colors and pillow backs. Instead, I learned the hard way by buying a sofa I hated from the moment it was delivered.

I do want you to take all sorts of fun risks in your home, but I want you to be smart about it so you aren't painting your grandmother's heirloom sideboard and regretting it. Or investing in a large piece before you truly know what you like and need. Begin with micro changes and tiny risks. It will give you a chance to learn what you like and why. You'll get familiar with colors and materials and skills before it matters all that much.

Do I think you should paint your fireplace? If you don't like it, yes. But I want you to practice by taking a baby step and painting something else first. ▪

7

You can't ruin something you already hate

THE ART OVER MY FIREPLACE on the cover of this book began its life at a big box store as a $49 canvas with a white globe printed on a black background. It's a recognizable piece of FART (factory-made art) that I bought for our son's room when we were doing a quick makeover.

After a few years, it had served its purpose and I was loading it up to drop off at Goodwill. I realized that if I ever needed a canvas that size, it would be cheaper to keep the FART and paint over it than go to the craft store and buy a new, empty canvas. A few weeks later I needed to fill a big wall, so I grabbed that canvas, put an old sheet under it to protect the floor, and gathered all the craft paint and cans of wall paint I had in the neutral colors I needed.

Over the course of a few days I poured, spattered, and layered paint on the canvas. Because I used my own wall paint, it looks great everywhere, so these days it gets moved around the house. This was the least risky DIY I've ever done in my life. Why? Because I had nothing to lose. I was going to literally give the canvas away. It was more work to drive the canvas to Goodwill than keep it. I basically took the lazy way out.

Before investing in a two-hundred-dollar dresser from Facebook Marketplace for your first ever makeover, asking your husband to drive across town to load it up, then painting it in the driveway in view of every curious neighbor—start with what you have. Learn in private without an audience who will question your every move.

Is there any little random piece of furniture in your garage, dining room, or attic that you've been giving dirty looks to because you hate the color? Start with that. Start with the thing that's already so not your style that the worst that could happen is you'll still dislike it. What if the best happens and you actually love it? ∎

8

One sane space

WHETHER YOU'RE MOVING into a new-to-you home, painting the family room, or beginning a major renovation, always provide one sane space for you and your family. This space is your temporary respite away from or in the midst of the chaos of change. It doesn't need to be finished, it just needs to be cozy and functional.

This is especially important if you are making changes to a room where you usually spend a lot of time. If you're painting the family room and that's where you gather every night to watch TV, it's worth it to make sure you can continue your routine. Perhaps you can keep the TV plugged in but pulled away from the wall and just uncover all the furniture at night. Or maybe the painting will take all week and the room needs to be empty. If so, consider setting up a temporary family room someplace else.

During major home transitions, I make it a point to show enthusiasm and excitement.

I learned this the hard way. If I complain and fret about everything the entire time I'm trying to transform a space, I'll dread the next change. If others bear the brunt of my woes, they'll dread the next change too. This is the opposite of what I want.

I want everyone to know that getting to make changes in our home, although intrusive and sometimes hard, makes me very happy. And the best way I know to do that is to be happy about it as it's happening. Does that mean I pretend to love something if I really hate it? No, but it means I verbally tell my family how grateful I am to get to try new things in our home.

When making changes in your home is fun and exciting for everyone, all will enjoy it. When making changes in your home is a pain and disrupts everyone's routine, including yours, all will dread it and you'll put off making changes until you have perfect circumstances, which will be never. My hope for you is that making changes in your home will become second nature, simple, fun, and something your family sees as a good thing that ultimately allows them to enjoy home even more. ■

Start at the heart and work your way out

TEN YEARS AGO we bought a fixer-upper on twelve overgrown acres. There were fourteen outbuildings, something furry and dead floating in the green pool, popcorn ceilings, a basement that leaked, weird wallpaper borders, pee-stained carpet, dilapidated outdoor pathways, a kitchen begging for mercy, and bathrooms with yellow bathtubs. The house was small, but the property was overwhelming. Where in the world would we begin?

My uncle Tracy is in landscaping, and when he stopped by to see our new place, he told us when the time came to tackle the outside, the best way to do it was to start at the house and work our way out. We clung to that advice over the years, and when we began a few outside projects, we started at the front and back doors, moving our way out. It worked! The changes we made were instantly visible and could be enjoyed every time we came and went. Over time we slowly worked our way outward from the house.

When Tracy visited, we were in the midst of years' worth of work that needed to be done in the house, so I wondered how we could apply his tip to the great indoors. When everything in a home seems to need equal attention, and when things are functional but just look bad, I've learned one way to make progress is to start at the heart of the home and work my way out. You get to decide what the heart is for you. For us it's usually the kitchen because we like to eat, I like to cook, and in our last few homes the kitchen was located in the middle of the house like a central hub where we all wanted to hang out. In our current home, the heart or center is the big foyer that spans the length of the house upstairs and down.

My usual routine when in a new home is to quickly set up **one sane space** (#8), address any floating furry things in the pool, take up the pee-stained carpet and paint the subfloor, then focus on the heart of the home and work my way out from there. If you've lived in your home for ages and it all feels overwhelming, same idea: start at the heart and work your way out. When you focus on the heart first, the changes are the most impactful and rewarding. ■

10

Minimal is a form of enough

I USED TO BELIEVE that the only people allowed to be minimalists are twentysomething bachelors with black leather sofas and no drapes. Or people who wear a daily uniform without being asked and count how few possessions they have and then brag about it to the rest of us hoarders. To me, minimalism was a harsh, colorless contemporary style that I didn't think of as pretty but that secretly sounded freeing. Oh well—the drab modern lines simply weren't for me, so cue the cute stuff!

Now it makes me sad that minimalism sometimes has a negative connotation. I get it—we equate the word *minimal* with the idea of barely adequate, just squeaking by, and even suffering. In reality, minimal is a form of enough. It's enough to meet a goal without excess. I don't know about you, but there are some areas of life where minimal is actually a better path than abundance.

Minimalism is not a style. It's a tool that helps us meet a goal.

You can use the minimal amount of decor and achieve any style, from Victorian to Farmhouse to Steampunk to Modern. If minimal means enough to meet a goal, and you get to decide what the goal is for your home, then minimal simply helps you know when to say "when." My personal goal when it comes to decorating is to get the maximum amount of style out of the minimum amount of stuff. I'm intentional about everything in my home because I want it to count.

We are better stewards of our resources, homes, and the world when we ask ourselves if we can get the same results with less. Less effort. Less money. Less time. Less stuff. When it comes to creating home, more isn't always better. And truly, enough is better than more. ■

Luxury isn't having more, it's needing less

THE FIRST TIME I heard someone say something like this, I knew they were lying. Luxury is having everything you might need or want at your fingertips, dummy.

One time when going on a ten-day trip to a new place far from home, I worried about what exactly I would need. So I packed every possible item. I even packed a million snacks, every medication in existence, and extra clothes in case this place had a hundred-year flood or freak cold front or heat wave. I was ultra prepared for anything.

My suitcase was a huge burden to me the entire trip. I couldn't quickly find what I was looking for, and I never even used 50 percent of what I lugged around. Who's the dummy now?

I was envious of my fellow travelers who had packed light. How luxurious to only carry what you know you'll need because you trust if something comes up unexpectedly you can figure it out!

This is reframing luxury. I now try to apply this to my home.

For the first time in our marriage Chad and I have a huge bedroom. It's embarrassingly gigantic. When we closed on the house, this huge empty room felt like the most luxurious space I'd ever been in, but not because it had gold foil ceilings or expensive wood floors. Nope! The doors in this century-old room didn't properly close (still don't), and the floor molding was (and still is) peeling. It was luxurious simply because of the extra space.

I knew I wanted to keep that feeling, and the best way was to have the barest of essentials so the room would stay functional and beautiful. It's tempting to add a gallery wall or more chairs "because I can," but then I'd lose that rarest of luxuries: empty space. To this day our bedroom is the most luxurious room in our home, not because of what it has but because of what it doesn't have: chaos, excess stuff, and clutter.

I could stare at this empty wall all day. It's like a microvacation for the eyes.

12

Admire, don't acquire

AS I SCROLL around the internet, flip through design books, and surround myself with beautiful inspiration, it can lead to feeling like I simultaneously have too much and not enough.

Suddenly I realize how much I love color and pattern and so many different styles and eras and the inspiration is overloading me and what is my style anyway? In the exact same moment I see beautiful items creatively paired together, I also feel like I have chosen poorly. Everything I have is wrong or incomplete or ugly and I need all new things yesternow. I have too much of the wrong stuff and not enough of the right stuff.

Wisdom is learning to appreciate things without trying to own them.

The beautiful empty field in front of our house that the neighbors own, the luscious fall decor overflowing the mantel in the magazine photograph, the latest trend all over Instagram—sometimes I wish those things were mine. But I'm also secretly relieved that I don't have to care for the extra property, pack away bins of plastic fall decor, or keep up with the latest trend if I don't want to.

Much of the joy of beautiful things can be found in simply recognizing and appreciating their beauty. Admiring something doesn't mean I need to be on a quest to have it. I'm allowed to like something without trying to make it mine. You're allowed to like something without trying to make it yours.

Acquiring comes with responsibilities that never show up in photos. ◼

Cozy doesn't mean cluttered

FOR THE FIRST HALF of my life I believed cozy was a style. MY style. I knew that layers of welcoming pillows, stacks of great books, and collections of cute tchotchkes had the power to transform a home from dull to delightful. The problem was, I didn't know how to stop at being delighted. So I added and added more items until I reached diabolical. My surfaces were overflowing with pretty things, and my small house felt chaotic and stressful.

Do you know that too much of anything can be awful? There is such a thing as a cozy threshold, and it's important for those of us who love beautiful objects to know when we've crossed it.

Like minimal, cozy is a tool, not a style. Pockets of abundance in our house can be magical spaces, but if every inch of our home is filled with an abundance of stuff, we're defeating the entire purpose of *home*.

I want the daybed in my office to hold comfy pillows and cozy throws, ready to welcome a weary soul for a quick lie-down or a nap. It's hard for someone like me, who could easily be a pillow hoarder, to not add more and more pillows until there's no room for an actual human. When I use coziness as a tool to help me reach a goal, I have a stopping point. If I want my daybed to be a place to lie down and rest, then there needs to be space for a person to actually do so. It might look fun if I have twelve pillows on the daybed, but it's not actually that welcoming since you need to hire a part-time pillow mover in order to use the daybed.

In our family room, I'm careful to limit our sofa pillows to two or three. I always want room for two people to sit down without first needing to resituate a pile of pretty pillows and throws. The cozy factor comes in with adding beautiful, useful, decorative pillows. The minimal factor comes in by adding just enough to meet the goal and no more. ■

14

Having it all is a lot to keep clean

THERE'S A DOWNSIDE to getting everything you want. At least that's what I tell myself since I don't have it all yet. Most of us fall into one of two camps when it comes to home decor: we are either overbuyers or underbuyers. This one's for the overbuyers—those of us who have a closetful of extra decor, just in case.

First, let me pay my respects to my fellow overbuyers. I understand that most of us are not overbuying high-end decor at full price every weekend. Nope. Most of us are overbuyers because at some point we had to make do. We had to be resourceful. Our collection of stuff—especially secondhand, has-so-much-potential stuff—happened over a long period of time and started from the noble goal of being a good steward.

For me, finding decor at a good deal started off as a necessity, a way to help cozy up our empty house on a budget. The problem was, I didn't know when to stop. It became a habit to run into a thrift store and look for the best stuff, feel great for only spending three dollars on a lamp, and then get home and realize I didn't actually need said lamp now, but it

was a great deal and if I painted it I might be able to use it someday. Look at me, saving so much money as I buy stuff I don't need and store it away forever just in case! I didn't understand that **luxury isn't about having more** (#11).

What started out as a useful skill never had a stopping point.

It wasn't until I realized that there was an actual cost to owning stuff and storing it that I stopped overbuying. I had clogged up my closets, drawers, and shelves with great deals that were cute and *almost* my style. Because my highest value was buying stuff on the cheap, I never questioned spending only three dollars on something cute. But spending three dollars ten times for items I didn't absolutely love meant not purchasing that one thirty-dollar item that I really wanted and needed.

I made decisions completely backwards, afraid that I would end up with nothing if I didn't collect the okay stuff at a bargain price. I learned to trust that I would be provided for and that if I was so great at finding good deals, I could find them in the future if needed.

If you find yourself stuck in the habit of collecting good-enough deals, ask yourself if you've hit a threshold and if shopping in the way you've always shopped is still serving you well. ■

15

It doesn't have to be perfect to be beautiful

"BEAUTY DOES NOT equal perfection." "Perfectly imperfect." "Embrace the imperfections." Yada, yada, yada. We've heard those expressions so often that we've become brain-blind to them. I wrote an entire book about welcoming imperfections, and I still struggle with accidentally believing perfection is the ultimate goal in every part of life.

But if the first step to making any change in your home is having the right goal (it is), and if somewhere deep inside you still secretly feel the pressure to pursue perfection, then it's imperative that you decide to choose to possibly consider that imperfection can actually help you reach your goal more than perfection.

Think about a time you've been the most comfortable in someone's home. Maybe it was a quick drop-in visit, a weekend stay, or dinner with a neighbor. On a scale of one to ten, what was the level of perfection and fanciness the host displayed in their home, life, and conversation? I'd bet the number you'd give is low. Perhaps the level was not even memorable. The truth is, we aren't super comfortable around people, homes, or circumstances where perfection is the expectation. We actually find ourselves drawn to the opposite because imperfection humanizes. Imperfection puts people at ease. Having a goal of hospitality leads to connection.

I've even learned to seek out the imperfect. When it came time for me to choose new counters in our kitchen, I was nervous but went with marble. I knew it would be beautiful, at least at first, but I had heard stories of people disappointed with how marble ages. It's soft, it scratches, and it discolors if you're not careful. I am not careful. I decided to see the aging of marble as a good thing, a sign of a good life in our kitchen with people to cook for and gatherings to host. It worked. I think it looks better with character.

There are so many other ways beautiful imperfection shows up in our home: scratches on the leather sofa, the crooked upstairs landing that we don't apologize for, permanent fingerprints on the unlacquered brass lamp. And the main way I've learned to show others that we don't expect perfection is by opening up our home before it's finished. In the midst of renovation, making decisions, painting rooms, or just waiting for a budget or inspiration. Letting people see this side of things builds connection between us.

Perfection isn't my goal, beautiful IMPERFECTION is. May it be yours as well. ■

16

Be your own house whisperer

AS SOMEONE who tries to make a living off creative endeavors, I've learned a lot about what I expected my job to entail and what it actually became. Before I dropped out of design school, I had this lofty vision of becoming a designer who dressed ultra cool. I would probably wear oversized glasses, carry flat leather portfolios to jobs in glass buildings, and create interesting spaces that wowed the masses.

Now that I'm doing creative work—the kind that looks nothing like what I thought (why don't I just try to dress cool anyway?)— I've learned the secret to getting my creative work done. If I had to narrow my job down to one thing that everything else would fall under, it would be to *keep myself inspired*.

When I'm inspired, all the other stuff happens easier, faster, and more naturally. When I'm uninspired, my work feels impossible. I've found this applies to anything I try to do.

When I apply that to creating home, I've learned the best way to keep on track of doing what I know, using what I have, and finishing what I start isn't comparison, negative self-talk, or deadlines. It's to be my own encourager, my own house whisperer. My *one job* is to seek out inspiration and the rest goes almost magically smooth. While the everydayness of work can make inspiration feel like a luxury you earn by completing a project, it's actually the *fuel* you need to finish the project.

The work is keeping yourself in the zone. It's the most important thing. Sometimes that means saying no to good but distracting things. Sometimes that means flipping through a shelter magazine, watching HGTV, or unfollowing someone on Instagram. As your bossy big sister who's been there and done that, I assure you that to prioritize putting yourself in scenarios where you'll experience beauty, art, risk, surprise, emotion, story, creation, and joy is vital to your creative work.

You can hire someone to paint your walls, hang wallpaper, and refinish your floors. But unless you are going to hire a designer, your ultimate job is to provide the vision for your home. No one else can do it for you. If you want to stay fresh for your creative work, your one job is to stay inspired, which comes with a secret perk: **inspiration leads to motivation** (#17). ◼

Inspiration leads to motivation

One of the first photos I ever saved on Pinterest was a round table packed full of plants. After ten years I finally got to re-create the look.

HAVE YOU EVER VISITED a beautifully decorated Christmas show house full of amazing ideas and you couldn't wait to get home and make a few changes to your own home? Or maybe you've walked through the aisles of a carefully curated antique mall, styled and staged to invite you to look for a while. The vignettes were so pretty, you got out your phone and took photos so you could re-create some tablescapes at home. Perhaps you went to your neighbor's house after she'd just painted a piece of beautiful furniture, and you remembered how awful it looked before. You suddenly wondered if you could paint the piece in your foyer and decided to buy some paint.

A natural result of inspiration is motivation.

Yes, knowing that guests are arriving tomorrow is also a form of motivation. But sometimes as we're making decisions in our home and getting stuck and feeling the womp womps of the unmotivated, we need something more than the prospect of being embarrassed to move us forward. We need positive, pure motivation, and it's at its finest when it happens naturally.

Use this knowledge as a secret weapon. Pay attention to what inspires you! When you need motivation, don't try to work up the gumption on your own. Simply seek out inspiration and let the motivation flow. ■

HOUSE RULES IN ACTION: 15 It doesn't have to be perfect to be beautiful 20 Respect your boss 29 Know your splurges and don't-cares 32 It doesn't have to be symmetrical to be balanced 41 Pair famous couples in design 43 Count every chair and prioritize tushies 49 The floor is lava 52 Layer your light 56 Twins, not friends 64 Contrast is queen if you want to be seen 71 Get your greens 74 Aim for home base 93 Add a spoonful of sugar

Your willingness to begin without perfect circumstances is your most valuable resource.

18

Clarity creates confidence

MOST OF THE STUDENTS I get to help as they make decisions about their home lack one thing. It's not a reasonable budget, and it's not creative ideas—it's simply the confidence to see their creative ideas through. My job is mainly telling people their idea is a good one and yes, they should do that!

One way to create your own confidence is to focus on getting really clear about your goals, priorities, and options. When you know what you want, how you want it, and how to get it, confidence naturally builds.

One sign that you don't have confidence is when you are asking advice from every person in your life. Maybe you are trying to decide on a paint color and have no idea what family of colors to even consider. Every human's opinion is up for grabs. Is the cable guy stopping by? What color does he think you should paint the room?

If you are doing this, stop. Remember, you want to get advice from people doing the thing you want to do in the way you want to do it. **You want a mindset you can model** (#2). Unless you've seen the cable guy's house, his opinion on your paint colors is useless.

The first step is to gather inspiration to help you figure out what you want. There's no one magic color, and deciding on paint isn't a pop quiz with a right or wrong answer. It's an art form that you discover as you consider how you want to use the room, what you want the room to feel like, and what existing colors in the room get a say in what colors will work for that space as you **respect your boss** (#20). Once you know the color family—a blue? a taupe? a blush?—then yes, there's usually a shade of that color that is ideal for your particular room.

Become very familiar with how you want to use the room and what activities need to happen there, and collect inspirational photos of rooms that feel like how you want your room to feel. I like to use Pinterest for this stage. The more time you spend homing in on what you really want and need, the more your confidence will quietly build in the background. ■

19

Every home has a silver lining

I'VE NEVER MET A HOME that doesn't have potential. Every home has something unique that can be played up, something wonky that can be turned into a delight, and something redeeming that is worth your time.

When you see a corner of a home featured in a magazine, the photo usually focuses on a special feature unique to the house. More than likely this feature started out as a limitation—and as you've learned, **limitations lead to innovations** (#3). Taking the logical course, that means the more limitations your home possesses, the more opportunities for creative solutions. Lucky!

I promise, there is so much hope for every home, for every circumstance. I believe there are always creative solutions that, when found, can make a home better than it would have been had the limitation not been there in the first place.

I zero in on finding the good in my own home by choosing to find something I like in every room, no matter what. Even if it's just "this room has a south-facing window" or "this room is cozy and warm in the winter." Whenever I begin to make changes in my home, I always begin by reminding myself of what I like about the space.

Instead of focusing on all that's lacking, gratitude puts us in a better mindset to begin a project in the home. Every room and every home has a silver lining. What's yours?

20

Respect your boss

NINE YEARS AGO we moved into a fixer-upper, and the very first thing I noticed were the orangey wide-plank pine floors. I also immediately noticed the hunter green walls, wallpaper borders, and red brick fireplace. All in one little room. There was a lot going on.

I didn't know exactly what I wanted, but I knew what I didn't want. So we immediately neutralized the walls and fireplace by painting them white. That left me with one strong statement element in the space: the pine floors.

What I didn't realize when we bought the house was that those wood floors were now the boss of me. By purchasing the house with the orange floors, I had entered into an unwritten contract with them. The green walls and brick were bosses too, but I chose to change those. Neutralizing them meant they couldn't boss me in the same way.

But the floors. Having a house full of beautiful, loud, orangey, leathery floors meant I couldn't just do whatever I wanted. I had a boss that demanded to be respected. I had two options: keep them and work with them, or change them. The one thing I couldn't do was ignore them.

Time and time again I see folks ignoring their house bosses.

Maybe you have wood cabinets with a yellow undertone. Instead of working with that color palette or changing it, you've chosen to ignore the color and pretend it doesn't exist. Then you try forcing your favorite color or trend to work with something it was never meant to. You end up unhappy and annoyed.

Learn to recognize if your space has a boss. Some do, some don't.

A boss could be a patterned green sofa you are keeping, a brick fireplace you love (or hate), a flooring color like pink carpet or gray tile, or dark wood trim. When you choose to live in a place that has built-in bosses, you are committing right then and there to either submit to those bosses or change them. Those are your only two choices.

So if you have pine floors like mine, they will boss or limit what colors you might use on the walls. If you have dark wood millwork, it's bossy. If you have a red brick fireplace, meet your boss.

I encourage you to work with the bosses that you love and don't try to work with a boss you absolutely hate. I might not have chosen orangey pine floors, but I knew I was up for the challenge of working with them. One way or another, you will need to respect your boss. ■

21

Style is found in the combinations

ALL OF DECORATING is about relationships. Relationships are created across all aspects of every decision you make: color, pattern, scale, shape, and so much more. Sometimes when decorating truths get a little woo-woo, I'll compare it to styling an outfit. Hear me out.

Have you ever purchased a new pair of jeans, maybe with a fresh silhouette or cut that you don't usually wear? That's great. But jeans alone don't create a style. Your personal style begins to show up the moment you pair the jeans with another piece like a top. More opportunities to create a unique style happen as you make more choices and add to your outfit, maybe with booties, earrings, and an overcoat. The more unexpected your style, the more surprising the pairings. The safer your style, the more predictable the pairings. Having a risky or funky style isn't right or wrong. It's just information for you to use and apply to your own options.

This concept is the same for decor. People will ask me how to mix styles in their home, and the very first step is to actually own indi-

vidual items with an instantly obvious style. You can't mix styles if nothing you own possesses an identifiable style. Let me be clear: if you want others to recognize that you're mixing styles, you have to mix items with a recognizable style.

In your wardrobe that might mean pairing bootcut jeans with stilettos, a slouchy white tee, and a worn leather moto jacket. In your room that might mean a modern white tulip table paired with a couple of masculine tufted vintage leather wingback chairs, and a classic tuxedo-style slipcovered daybed with old wood shutters and a Mouille-style floor lamp. Now we've got a unique style achieved by mixing styles. Phew!

Anyone can have good taste by purchasing something that looks great alone. But style requires you to create combinations. Combining different eras, silhouettes, textures, colors, sizes, and contrasts creates style possibilities. That means if you desire a mix of styles in your home, you'll want to include individual items that have a strong, identifiable style and presence.

Unique style requires unique combinations. Classic style requires classic combinations. Quirky style requires quirky combinations. The possibilities are endless, and you get to decide what you like.

Pieces with presence combined together create a personalized style. ◼

See House Rule 13 for the other side of this room.

22

Test it before you invest in it

THE FIRST TIME I had the opportunity to renovate a kitchen was exciting and terrifying. It's one thing to choose a pillow, lamp, or chair that can be returned or sold if I end up hating it. It's an entirely different thing to choose cabinets, counters, and hardware.

We were tearing down walls and deciding cabinet locations from scratch, and I needed help visualizing my choices so I could have more confidence. So, once I figured out what I thought was the best island layout and taped down an outline on the floor, I moved a nearby dresser to the kitchen, then gathered a bunch of big empty moving boxes and planted them side by side. By mocking up the size and shape of the island, I could get a sense of what it felt like in the room. I was able to walk around it and feel if it was the right scale for the space.

I was also considering a commercial-style faucet, one of those tall gooseneck things with coils around it and a pull-down sprayer.

Again, this was new to me and I wanted a visual of how it would look in the space. Would the height bother me and be annoying in the middle of the island? To help me make a decision, I found an umbrella with a curved handle reminiscent of the gooseneck faucet and duct-taped it to the placeholder dresser I had mocked up as an island, making sure to raise it to the height the faucet would stand so I could be as informed as possible.

Did my mocked-up island look ridiculous? Yes. Was I hoping my husband wouldn't walk in and see what I was doing? Absolutely. Did it help me make more confident decisions? One hundred percent.

Other ways I've created ridiculous-looking scenarios that helped: Moving a tiny table to the center of our foyer to see if I liked having a table there. Painting multiple walls in our house to be sure of the color before the professionals came in and actually painted for real. And purchasing a little throw rug in the same style as a large rug I'm considering to see if the colors work in the room so I don't have to lug a 10×14 rug back to the return line.

The more expensive, invasive, and permanent a change, the more it's worth finding a way to test it first. ■

23

Find your own timeless classics

TWENTY-SEVEN YEARS AGO I purchased a simple white Bassett dresser for $350 from JCPenney to use in the nursery as a changing table and storage for our firstborn son. Since then, as we've moved to different houses, that dresser has been put to various uses. In the kitchen as storage. At the back door as a drop zone. In our bathroom to hold towels. Back to a bedroom as an actual dresser. Into the foyer as a pretty landing area. In our family room to store DVDs we never watch. And at the moment it's in my closet.

Years ago I gave it a fresh coat of white paint, but besides needing a bit of repair on one or two of the drawers, which I'm sure we won't actually get to, this dresser has remained unchanged.

This, ladies and gentlemen, is one of my timeless classics.

Over the years, in all our houses built in different eras and styles, throughout all the trends and my own personal style changes, this humble white dresser has always been able to fit right into the decor and serve us well. I keep loving it and using it and not hating it, and that's something to pay attention to.

Your timeless classic might be a specific piece of furniture like my dresser. Or perhaps it's a silhouette that you've always loved like a wingback chair. Maybe it's a pattern you never tire of like houndstooth or stripes or toile. Maybe you loved mixing metals with your jewelry in high school and you're still mixing metals today in your home with accessories and hardware. If there's a fabric that always feels right to you—velvet or denim or linen or leather or hide—pay attention to that.

No matter what your timeless classics are, you've got to be aware of them. That way you can have extra confidence when making decisions, purchases, or changes in your home, knowing you're more likely to love and use something for the long haul if it incorporates items you have a history with. Often these timeless classics are the foundation for a soulful, personalized home that transcends the trends.

Take a few minutes to walk around your house right now and look for your own timeless classics.

What pieces have you had the longest and still love and use?

What style do you love no matter what the trends say?

What fabrics or patterns feel timeless to you, that you can always work into your home no matter what?

Discovering what you've been drawn to all along will help you hone your personal style, embrace its quirks, and make confident decorating decisions. Plus . . . it's fun! ■

24

Ignore the builder

OFTEN, THE HOME BUILDER'S JOB is to create what the masses expect and do that as quickly, simply, and inexpensively as possible to appeal to their ideal home-buyer. That makes great business sense, and unless you have a custom or older period home, understand that most of the things your builder included are *suggestions* and most likely haven't involved lots of personal modifications and considerations.

The kitchen faucet finish, island pendant style, front door color . . . suggestions. Most of us realize we have the freedom to change these things. However, one of the most powerful ways to make sure our homes are serving us is to evaluate the purposes of the rooms themselves. It's normal to do this when you first move in, but I want you to do this every few years as your needs change.

The room with the chandelier hanging low is the one the builder suggests would work as a dining room. The room above the garage with the built-ins is what the builder suggests for the home office. Once you move in, it's difficult to see past the purpose you first assigned to each room based on those suggestions. Three, four, ten years later you begin to feel your home isn't serving you and

you need to move. This might be the solution, but first it's important to evaluate each room in your house and how you are using it.

Our living room is lovely, with hundred-year-old millwork, a six-foot-wide pair of pocket doors, one wall with a double-hung window surrounded by built-ins, a corner fireplace, and three additional doorways to other rooms. Yep, you're right—there is almost no wall space. So I had to get creative and ignore what the builder might have expected when it came to furniture layout and the purpose of the room.

This house still has one working fireplace out of the five you can see, in addition to two that have been covered by drywall. A century ago this home was heated by coal-burning fireplaces; today, however, I need some of that wall space for seating and surfaces for people. My solution? A table and a pair of swivel chairs directly in front of one of the many fireplaces that haven't been used in years.

Think about what type of space or function your home is missing, then consider how much use each room in your home is currently getting. It might be that instead of moving, you simply need to rename your room or reconsider the original layout. The most delightful rooms in many homes are spaces that have been redesignated to suit the lifestyle, family needs, and personal obsessions of those who call the place home. ■

25

Plan on the kids growing up

WE HAD THREE BOYS in the span of three and a half years, and for ages our coffee table decor was a stiffly woven rectangular basket that perfectly held a stack of diapers and wipes with a leftover sliver of space for lotions and I think my nail polish. Nothing else. At the time I couldn't envision a future where I could choose something pretty to set on the coffee table.

If you are in that stage of life and it feels like it will never end? Well, that sounds about right. But of course it will end, and you already know to savor it if possible. You know you're in the "good old days," though they sometimes feel like they will go on relentlessly forever.

But when our kids are young, we sometimes make big, home-altering decisions as if they'll be tiny forever. We don't buy the house with bedrooms on two different levels. We avoid homes with stairs because we've got crawlers. We think we can't have drapes in any room because of toddlers. And maybe that's something to navigate for a series of months, but it's not going to define the rest of your life.

Beware of making long-term trade-offs in your home without considering what your life could look like in eighteen months. I'm that mom who let her boys ride bikes and rollerblades in the house (if we had the space), so take what I say with a grain of decorative salt. But if you have littles and feel stuck in your options, know that you'll have different options soon. Meanwhile, choose the prettiest diaper basket you can find. ■

Our youngest son is in college, and we had a great time making decorating decisions for his room together.

26

What's the third way?

ONE WAY TO MAKE CHANGES in your home is to come up with a plan and redo everything to your exact liking. If that is possible for you, congratulations! You are one of the lucky few.

For those of us who can't do that, we often assume we'll have to wait until circumstances change so that we can. And if we don't feel hopeful that will happen any time in the foreseeable future, we despair and end up giving dirty looks to each room as we do nothing.

When you're feeling stuck because that hard reality has hit you, it's easy to think it's the end of the road. To think you should wait until you win the lottery and have the funds to buy a house, move to a bigger home, or make some other form of a huge change from your current circumstances. If you can't do that . . . well, it must mean you can do nothing.

I have to work through this thought process for every room I work in.

We moved into our current house, and although the cabinets themselves weren't awful, the kitchen island had varying levels of surfaces combined with unnecessary angles. The counters were busy and outdated, and the wall and paint colors were thick and heavy.

I wanted a new kitchen, and we'd put some money aside for the project. We measured, received a reasonable quote from one of my favorite kitchen designers, and were excited about getting started. The first thing the designer wanted us to do was decide on the exact appliances we wanted to use in the space. Chad and I went appliance shopping and learned that all the appliances we were interested in were backordered. Not for a few months but for a year and a half.

Not only did I utter a few "why-mes" for obvious reasons, but I also knew I needed to take photos for this book in nine months. I couldn't photograph a kitchen with holes where the appliances should be.

When this happens you have to remember: It's not yes or no. It's not now or never. It's what CAN we do? What is the third way? Don't ask, "Is there a third way?" Assume there *is* one and it's your job to find it.

Luckily, Chad was on it and he asked what would happen if we focused on what we could change now. That question made all the difference. And it leads us to the next house rule: **add a temporary fix to the mix** (#27). ▪

27

Add a temporary fix to the mix

WHEN CIRCUMSTANCES don't enable you to do what you want but also don't allow you to wait for whatever is necessary to move forward, that means it's time for a temporary fix.

A temporary fix is anything that holds you over so a room serves you and looks better until you can do what you want or need to in the future.

When you decide to try a temporary fix, a pressure-reducing move, you often end up finding more creative solutions than you would have in the first place. This is due to the temporary nature of it, making it easier to take a risk. Plus, **you can't ruin something you already hate** (#7).

A temporary fix can be as simple as borrowing folding tables from church and putting drop cloths over them for a big family gathering, or as long-term as adding new counters on top of older cabinets.

For our kitchen, we decided on a temporary fix. We talked about how long we needed the temporary fix to work, how much we were willing to spend, what function needed to change, what we could live with, and which simple fixes would have a big impact.

We decided to aim for a temporary fix that would work for the next five years. That would get me through a few projects I needed to tend to, and then we could reevaluate. Our budget was 20 percent of what we had saved to do a total makeover, and we wanted to get it done in a matter of months.

Functionally, we decided to leave every cabinet in its place but extend and change the shape of the island. We chose new counters, sink, faucet, and lighting. After living with the appliances for a few months, I liked them. Although older, they worked great and were high-quality, so we kept them. Once all the changes were made, I decided on a paint color for the cabinets that instantly hushed and neutralized the kitchen; suddenly it was done and felt like our house.

Would I have loved a brand-new layout and custom cabinets? Of course. Do I love my kitchen now? Absolutely. I took a risk on mixing countertops with dark soapstone and light marble, had fun with lighting choices, and splurged on the kitchen faucet. Because these weren't forever choices, I felt freer to take a risk. I believe our kitchen came out 80 percent as good as if we had totally gutted it, but thanks to finding the **third way** (#26), it only cost us 20 percent of the money, took 10 percent of the time, and caused far less disruption to our lives. ■

28

Amateur guesstimate or professional estimate?

I HAD FINALLY DECIDED on a wall and trim color for our first floor, so I contacted our painter to come give me a cost estimate for the job. When he stopped by, I asked him on a whim if he could also quote the cost to paint our chimney's red exterior brick white to go with the rest of our house.

I had always assumed painting the chimney would be something we did once we won the lottery. To me it seemed like a HUGE gnarly job because that side of the house is already way higher than ground level, plus the chimney reaches crazy high next to our steeply pitched roof. With as hard as it was to get to, I was pretty sure it would be ridiculously expensive for them to paint it, but how could I decide not to do it if I didn't know how much it would cost?

It turns out it was crazy cheap to have the chimney painted.

Even though I know better than to give myself fake quotes and then make deci-

sions for my home based on my uneducated guesses, this is not the first time I've done this.

We had a gravel driveway forever and always dreamed of how exquisite it would be to have an actual paved driveway with dark black asphalt. But years ago a friend mentioned how much he thought it might cost to pave the driveway, and it was more than a year of college tuition. We kept that number in our heads as gospel, choosing never to pursue paving the driveway because we couldn't afford that much.

Years later a driveway company pulled up to our house and offered to measure and give us a free quote right on the spot, and Chad practically floated in to tell me the cost. It was less than half of what we imagined!

I keep having to learn the same lesson. Never change or postpone your plans or dreams based on what you assume something will cost. What if you're wrong?

Even if right now you have zero dollars budgeted for a project, getting an estimate on the cost will give you a realistic goal, is a wise first step, and will help you truly know if it's a project you can afford.

Whether it's renovating the kitchen, moving the chandelier, replacing the front door, landscaping the side of the house, or adding in the pool, don't assume you know how much it will cost.

You gotta get that quote so you can make informed decisions. ■

29

Know your splurges and don't-cares

I LOVE THOSE POLLS on social media where people ask what your personal splurge items are, things you're always willing to spend more on because the quality matters to you. You can learn a lot about a person from their answer. There's also the opposite question to consider: what things *don't* matter to you that you don't care to spend money on?

Although I will tell you what my splurges and don't-cares are when it comes to my home, it's more important for you to pay attention and learn what your own are. Why? Because there's no right or wrong answer. You get to decide what's important to you.

When it comes to furniture, I'm always willing to look for secondhand case goods—surfaces and storage usually made of wood or hard materials. If I need a bookshelf, dresser, or side table and can find it secondhand, that's a win. But for upholstered pieces—

sofas and chairs of all sorts—I am willing to splurge on new down-wrapped cushions and custom-made pieces because I **prioritize tushies** (#43) and we're sitting on these daily.

When it comes to art, I will spend money on original art from time to time, especially if I'm obsessed with the artist or style. But mostly I like unexpected, weird things on my walls, and if I have a gap in my wall art, I'll just make something abstract myself using an old canvas I already have with colors I know work in my house. Because there are **other ways to pay** (#31), the cost of finding great art I like for my walls is paid with my time and creativity. Either I'm looking for weird, cool, or funky secondhand items, or I'm making my own.

I've started letting myself splurge more on lighting, and let me tell you—it's worth the splurge. Lighting with a voice, with a unique style and presence, adds so much in both beauty and function. It makes me sad that I used to ignore that. So many missed opportunities!

As you're reading my splurges you're either nodding along in agreement or shaking your head in bewilderment. That's wonderful! The entire point is for you to get familiar with what matters to you, splurging where it counts and not caring about the rest. ■

I found the sideboard and mirror on Facebook Marketplace and the rug is from Amazon. The lamps, although secondhand, were the most expensive items in this picture.

30

Ask why

I'M LUCKY ENOUGH to have a dedicated room in my house for an office. But a few weeks ago I noticed that I've been grabbing my laptop and bringing it into the family room to work.

Yes, I could force myself to work in my office. Or I could become frustrated with myself because I just painted my office a few months ago so why am I not working there? But if I want every room to work for me and be fully used, the only way to create real change is to ask *why*.

Why don't I sit in my office? Well, because I want to sit in the family room. Why do I want to sit in the family room? Because it's cozier. Why is it cozier? Because in the winter I wake up early and it's dark outside and the family room has great task lighting and a cozy chair that I love sitting in and a warm fireplace that comes on at the flip of a switch. It feels private and cozy and protected. There it is! Actually helpful, meaningful information.

The vintage chairs in my office have flat cushions and straight backs, are made of stiff, cold leather, and are pulled against a cold marble-top table. The chair where I like to sit in the family room is made of cozy upholstery, swivels, and has high, flat, protective arms where I can set my phone, pens, and books.

The lighting in my office is made up of leftover lamps I couldn't find a place for in the rest of the house. In the morning the room is cold, the shutters on the windows don't close all the way, and I feel like people can look through the window and see me sitting there.

Lastly, the fireplace in the family room is like a magnet. Why would I choose not to sit in front of it at all times?

Asking why has led me to actionable changes I can make if I want to create an office I can use. I might not be able to add a fireplace, but there's a lot I can do. The truth is, when we moved here my office mostly got leftover pieces while the public rooms got dibs on the seating, surfaces, storage, rugs, lighting, and even my attention and budget. Before I asked why, I simply felt guilty that I was avoiding my office but didn't know what that meant. Now I'm clear on which problems to solve, and that keeps me going.

Remember, **when we have clarity and purpose, we find motivation and confidence** (#18).

31

Other ways to pay

MOST OF US ARE TAUGHT there is one way to pay for stuff, and the cost of everything is money. Have money? You win! You get a beautiful everything.

Wrong. Money is one way to pay, and we all understand how it works. But there are many ways to pay for things, and when it comes to creating a home you love and use, this can be great news. You can make big changes in your home even with no budget as long as you are willing to **be resourceful** (#5) and pay in other ways.

Let's say you don't like your bedroom but don't have the money to buy new stuff. Here are some other ways to pay.

Time. If you have the time, you can sell your bed and dresser on Facebook Marketplace, to a consignment store, or at a garage sale. Then you can use that money to search for other secondhand items and purchase things you love. If you have time, you can be the first one to the yard sale every Saturday and get the best deal. If you have time, you can pop into your local thrift stores on the weekly and score big. If you have time, you can be patient and wait for the right items.

Freedom. When you have freedom, you don't have to ask permission from your landlord to paint the walls. You can sell your furniture without convincing your partner or feeling guilty that someone will be mad. You can try something out and make a wrong choice because you've given yourself freedom to make a mistake.

Space. With space you can hold on to items you might need in the future—although I don't love this one because I have abused it. A garage full of stuff for "someday" and "just in case" still has a cost. But if used for a purpose, this can be a way to save up a few choice items for when you need them.

Creativity. The more creative you are willing to be, the more solutions you can find. Maybe you decide to wrap your existing headboard in foam and fabric to DIY a new-to-you upholstered headboard. Maybe you paint your dresser.

Although you can't print money, stop time, force freedom, or create space out of nothing, you can always conjure up some decorative currency in the form of creativity. It's the resource you have the most control over. ▪

32

It doesn't have to be symmetrical to be balanced

WE HAVE AN ODD NUMBER of children. This is a nonissue unless you are seating them in pairs on a roller coaster or your favorite piece of artwork happens to be a set of hand-cut silhouettes you had made by a silhouette artist. The latter was my dilemma.

I had recently upgraded the three silhouettes from their small frames and mats to something more substantial so they could get the attention they deserved when hung on our wall. I was totally **nailing that scale** (#39). The problem was, the wall where they would look best was tiny, awkward, and held an off-centered loveseat. If I hung these frames in either a horizontal or vertical line, they were too big. They'd also draw attention to the fact that the loveseat wasn't centered on the wall. What I really needed was an extra child so I could complete my even number of silhouettes and have four frames in two rows of two.

Yes, I could have purchased an extra frame and had a silhouette made of the dog or the house, or even a hand-lettered favorite verse or quote, but that didn't feel right to me. I secretly felt like that would be the easy way out, and this seemed like an opportunity to get creative. After all, we know **limitations lead to innovations** (#3)! So I hung up the three frames staircase style on the little wall over the loveseat and lived with it for a few days while staring at that empty space every free moment I had.

I knew the missing item needed to feel different from the square frames yet still relate to them. I wanted something unexpected. Then I remembered the wood ribbon art created by my friend and artist Angela Chrusciaki Blehm. One of the larger pieces could be exactly what I needed while solving a slew of problems creatively.

It WAS! The organic, flowy, off-center style of the ribbon art was the perfect, PERFECT funky partner to the framed silhouettes. And it allowed for my off-centered loveseat to have art centered above it but still honor the entire wall.

That awful area I had cursed and hated became the coziest, quirkiest, warmest, welcomingest corner in our home. And although it wasn't symmetrical, it *was* visually balanced. The same concept can be applied to your home: aim for balance, not symmetry. ▪

33

Just because it costs less doesn't mean you're saving money

IT WAS 2020 and everyone was home. The small-scale sofa I had ordered a few months earlier was just delivered. It was custom-made by a local furniture maker and was worth the wait. I instantly loved it and knew it was the right size for our home. And suddenly we had our college-age boys back at home, so seating was a priority.

I moved a few chairs in from another room, and they were comfy and worked fine. But next to my new sofa they showed their age. I knew I could have a second, smaller sofa custom-made to exactly fit the space where I needed it, but I didn't want to pay for that and wait six to eight weeks for my room to look better.

So instead, I ran directly to IKEA and purchased the smallest loveseat they had that I didn't hate, at less than half the cost of the custom piece I could have had made. The boys were glad to have a new place to sit, and the loveseat confirmed that a smaller sofa would work where I needed it. But I didn't love it. It was still six inches too long, and frankly, it looked bad. I told myself that settling for fast and cheap would make up for not getting exactly what we needed, but that was a lie.

I've learned that purchasing things that sort of work can be a huge waste of money. If I'm able, it's more responsible to save, be patient, and purchase the thing that works perfectly.

I ended up having a tiny sofa made for the little wall in our house, and it was worth every penny and every day I had to wait. I ordered a **timeless** (#34) English roll-arm sofa in a neutral color that I plan on using for many years, and it fit right in at our next house. And since it's a quality piece, I can have it re-covered if I ever change my mind about the fabric. I found another place in our house for the IKEA loveseat and bought a neutral linen slipcover so I could use it for years.

If you are patient, you're more likely to save money in the long run, save a piece from going to a landfill too early, and be happier with your purchase. Learn from my mistake.

As much as it pains my frugal mindset to admit it, sometimes the more expensive item can be the better value. ■

34

Timelessness is here to stay

IF YOU WANT to invest in something timeless, simply look back over the past few decades and notice what is still in use today. It's the same principle as finding your **personal timeless classics** (#23). Figure out clues by doing a Google image search of home decor from the 1960s, 70s, 80s, or 90s, or page through old magazines or decorating books from a secondhand store.

You'll have to train your eyes to ignore trends like colors, patterns, and even weird filters from old cameras, but then it's time to investigate, looking through the photos for timeless items. Here are a few questions to ask yourself as you work to spot them:

- If you had to choose some items, what could you incorporate into your home today?
- What items would fit with the style of your favorite store?
- What items have you seen in houses you admire?
- What silhouettes, materials, colors, patterns, and finishes are we still using today?

I'll go first. I'm using my treasured copy of Rachel Ashwell's *Shabby Chic* from 1996.

What do I see that I'd use in my house today? I see many things! One is a great little ball-and-claw-foot bench covered in a leopard print fabric. I'd use that!

What would fit with the style of my favorite store? I see a gilded gold mirror that I've seen in lots of stores. I just priced some online yesterday for our bathroom.

What items have I recently seen in houses I admire? I see dentil molding painted in a fresh white along with white slipcovered upholstery and a dark wood table. It reminds me of artist and designer Josh Young's classic home.

What silhouettes, materials, colors, patterns, and finishes are we still using today? There's a square tuxedo armchair like I have, just with different fabric, no channel stitching, and a ruffled skirt. Oh, and it's paired with an accent pillow that's taller than the back, so now I want to try that.

Pay attention to the timeless pieces you noticed. For me, it was furniture shapes and silhouettes like the square tuxedo chairs and ball-and-claw-foot bench. The square shape of the tuxedo chair can be incorporated into any style just by changing the fabric. The ball-and-claw motif has been around for hundreds of years. And God himself created leopard print. ■

35

Let it be easy

I HAVE A TENDENCY to overcomplicate things.

In his book *Effortless*, Greg McKeown asks readers, "What if this could be easy?" *House Rules* is a direct result of wondering how I could write the most helpful book in a way that didn't kill me. Long-form writing is my nemesis, so how could I make this easier?

But the principle applies to everything, especially while making decisions in your home. As you approach a project, ask yourself, What if this could be easy? What decisions would you make then? What would the outcome be? What's "easy" for you might seem difficult for others, so there's no wrong way to let something be easy, as long as it's easier for you (and legal).

Maybe you are a professional wallpaper installer and incorporating lots of wallpaper is easy for you. Great! Maybe you are a contractor and hiring people to create custom built-ins is so easy. Then do that. Maybe you love figuring things out and want to watch all the YouTube videos and do all the DIYs. You

go, girl. Often, the easy way is the way that makes us feel most confident, and there's nothing wrong with that.

I'm addicted to using neutrals. It's easy! I'm lazy . . . and also smart! I've learned that I'm too finicky when it comes to colors, but I love silhouettes, textures, mixed metals, and woods. So the easier way for me is to stick to neutrals in my home. It's the KISS concept (keep it simple, stupid) in action. The simpler you keep it, the less possibility there will be for mistakes.

When we moved into our current home, the family room was painted a dark green with taupe trim. All the custom shutters were painted the same color as the trim. In the spirit of letting it be easy, I kept the original trim color and had the walls painted white. That way we didn't have to deal with the pain of painting working shutters. Easy.

Letting it be easy might mean deciding to purchase the same sofa as your sister-in-law because you already know you love hers. It might mean painting every wall on the main level the same color because you already know it looks good with your floors. **When it doubt, carry it out** (#57)! Letting it be easy often begins with simply doing what you already know. ■

USE WHAT YOU HAVE

ONE BY ONE over the course of a few years our boys were graduating from high school and going off to college and trade school. It was time for me to finally get my lady sofa. For years our existing sectional sofa had faithfully taken a beating and provided so much needed seating (and surprisingly still looked decent), but I was ready for a change.

It was tempting to just haul out the old sofa and start with an empty room, but it still had one last job to do. One way to figure out what you need and want is by using what you have to evaluate what is and isn't working. This is a valuable step. Before you go buy something new, begin with what you already have.

I wanted to experiment with where a smaller sofa could work in our tiny family room. So I detached the two pieces of the sectional, pushed one onto the porch, and used the other as a placeholder. I was able to try my half sofa out on every wall. I brought in a few random chairs from other rooms and used them as placeholders too. I was planning to keep the same coffee table and TV console, but I went to the trouble of unplugging the television and moving everything around until I found a layout that worked.

The room looked utterly ridiculous but the practice was endlessly helpful. I found a surprising furniture layout with the sofa centered in front of the windows. Once I knew my layout, I could see that the sofa section I was using was too long and covered vents under each window. So I then had a maximum sofa length I could shop for. I wanted the coffee table in line with the fireplace and also centered on the sofa, which gave me a maximum sofa depth to allow for enough room between the sofa and table. I also wanted a sofa with a slightly lower back that would not block out so much natural light from the window. My old sofa provided a lot of valuable information about what I did and did not want: I now had ideal dimensions that helped inform the style I needed and wanted.

This is one way of using what you have. Whether it's understanding what's missing in a room, recognizing what is already there, or being positive about what you don't want, evaluating what you have is a must. Don't dismiss the pieces you've had forever and how they can be incorporated in a new way or provide helpful information for your next purchase.

I hope the tips in this section will help you evaluate if and how you can use what you already have in all sorts of different ways. And if there's something you can't use, I hope you'll be able to pass it on with confidence, knowing exactly what you need to replace it.

36

Quiet the house

OVER TIME I find myself slowly adding in layers of coziness to every room of our house—a few extra pillows and throws on the sofa, a stack or two of books on the shelf, an extra candle here and there. By the time a few months pass, my surfaces are overflowing with excess coziness and cute clutter, and I kind of forget what my room truly looks like naked.

Everything in your room has a voice, and some voices are louder than others. A bright-red, chunky mirror has a visually louder voice than the white taper candle that sits on your dresser, but both have a voice that takes up visual, physical, and even emotional space in your room.

Most of us add things, but rarely do we take time to purposely remove stuff from our house and undecorate it. Quieting your space removes all those voices from a room at once. It requires that the cute decorative stuff you've become house-blind to proves its worth before it comes back in.

Instead of holding every item and assigning an emotional rating to it, or mercilessly evaluating every individual item one by one, I just remove it all! This gives an instant reward of experiencing my house with less, and then I wait twenty-four hours to let it sink in. After experiencing a room without clutter, I'm naturally pickier about what should come back into it. It's a simple way I trick myself into letting go of things, and it works every time.

When it comes to decluttering visual decor, don't start by making individual decisions; start by experiencing the result of a decluttered room. It's backwards decluttering.

Here's how to quiet your house in five simple steps:

1. Pick one room to quiet. Yes, the rule says to quiet the house, but we're technically working one room at a time.
2. Find a temporary holding place to put the stuff you'll remove from your room. Anywhere out of the room you're quieting works.
3. Remove all the knickknacks, gewgaws, little junk, tchotchkes, and decorative smalls. If you need a bigger change, remove everything from your walls too—even the drapes.
4. Let your space breathe for at least twenty-four hours so you can reconnect with it.
5. Only bring back things that you really love, miss, and need. Get rid of the rest. Don't fill a space just because it's empty. ■

37

Does your room look good naked?

SOMETIMES WHEN I'm frustrated with a room I tend to blame my furniture layout, the chair that isn't my very favorite, the latest tchotchke I purchased from Target, my personal budget . . . you get the idea. But many times the underlying reason I don't love a room is because I'm starting from a canvas that doesn't represent my style at all.

When you **quiet your house** (#36) you're able to reexperience your room in a more pure state stripped of all the cute stuff that can distract you from what's truly happening in it. You'll notice parts of your room that were there all along—things like paint color, repairs that need attention, built-ins, millwork, window style, mantel and fireplace surround, flooring, and ceiling style. These all have an impact on your room. If you dislike a lot of the choices in any room of your house, you'll have a little more work to do getting the room to a place where it feels like you. Remember to **respect your bosses** (#20) and either work with them or decide now what can be changed.

Most of us can't completely renovate a room's style from top to bottom. But if you don't love your room when it's naked, consider what you can change, upgrade, DIY, or make over to help update and upgrade the bones of the room. Changing out a light fixture or hardware, adding millwork or beams, updating the flooring, or simply getting a bigger rug to hide flooring you don't love are worthwhile changes with big payoff. And don't underestimate the power of painting the walls, ceiling, or trim and updating a fireplace.

When done thoughtfully, these changes add to the value of your home, keep your personal style from being sabotaged by someone else's past choices, and allow you to use fewer decorative items to achieve the look you want. Creating a room that looks good naked is more work, but the payoff is bigger and **you get to choose your trouble** (#89).

When we rented homes, I had to be more creative in some ways because I couldn't permanently change the bones of a room. Switching out overhead lights, painting, and adding rugs over flooring I didn't love helped a lot.

It's more work to decorate a room when you don't love it empty; it's easier to decorate a room when it looks great naked. This doesn't mean you can't love a room that you don't like naked—just be prepared to work a little harder. ◼

38

Shop the house

YOU HAVE ACCESS to a personally curated collection of goods at your fingertips—your own house—and it's full of possibilities.

Treating your house like a shop is the simplest, least risky way to try out a new idea. Maybe you're considering adding a soft cushy upholstered chair at either end of your dining table. You don't want to go out and purchase two big soft cushy upholstered chairs, lug them home, then see if you like them. No, you first shop your house. You walk through every room looking for a chair (or pair of chairs) you can try at the end of your table for zero dollars to see if you like them. From there you get even more information: do you like this color, height, shape, arm style? This gives you confidence to make a better decision. Shopping your house is one way to **test it before you invest in it** (#22) and a great way to begin to use what you have.

Shopping your house is also an ideal way to verify that every decorative item you own is in the best possible place. Imagine you just

purchased a vase. You walk in the back door, set it down on the kitchen island, and . . . bam! It looks magnificent! Then you try it on the dining room table and . . . darn it! It looks amazing there too! No worries. You don't get overwhelmed; you get excited knowing that you've hit the decorating jackpot and now you get to try this vase everywhere. You want to see where it's needed the most or where you enjoy it the most. What a fun quest! A few months later, when you find a new-to-you coffee table, you are excited to shop your house first, trying the vase on the coffee table to see if that's the best place for it.

Many people are afraid to shop their own house because they assume if they like the way something looks, they don't want to risk messing with it. But understand that just because something looks good doesn't mean it couldn't look even better. Your stuff is there to serve you, and you want to make sure you get full enjoyment out of it.

If you're worried about removing a piece from a pretty vignette, snap a quick photo and remember: you have a very generous, no-fuss return policy in your own shop. It's your house. Everything can instantly be put back where you found it, and everything is up for grabs. ■

39

Nail that scale

LET ME INTRODUCE you to America's biggest faux pas: decorating with stuff that's too small.

Scale—the size of an object compared to its surrounding context—is something we collectively just can't seem to get right.

When we use an item that is too small, we naturally realize it looks weird. But instead of deciding to change out the small item for something larger, for some crazy reason our natural tendency is to ADD MORE small items. We see this phenomenon play out on styled gallery walls, sofas, beds, mantels, and coffee tables, and it affects everything from lamp choices to the scale of furniture in a large room.

My leather cigar sofa is eighty-nine inches wide. For a sofa, it's on the small side. But even my smallish sofa deserves an anchor pillow or two that has impact, pillows with a decent scale. See how using tiny pillows, even though they're pretty, feels cluttered, and how adding more isn't the best solution?

Instead, look at what happens when I add a large, twenty-seven-inch pillow in the corner. That's more like it. Now I can use smaller pillows as extras if I want to, but starting with the right scale changes everything.

The same goes for a mantel. If you start with something like a piece of art that's too small, you'll probably end up adding an abundance of small items in an effort to fill space. If you're like me, you'll fall into the trap of believing that if you can just add the right combination of small items, you'll finally figure it out. But the truth is, a few large items have more impact than many smalls.

Maybe you've tried to style your coffee table and can't get the combination of things just right. One no-brainer solution is to pick just one item, like a plant and container, and scale it up. Now it looks amazing, risky, and has a bigger impact thanks to using one large item.

The scale of your lighting should relate to the scale of the seating it's near and the surfaces it sits upon. Too often a big king-size bed flanked by matching nightstands gets tragically paired with wittle bitty twelve-inch baby lights barely fit for a dorm room. Or a large overstuffed sofa will have a wimpy little plant stand next to it. Yes, I want you to **combine the opposites** (#62), but when it comes to scale, most of your items still need to relate.

If you have a problem area in your home that you just can't figure out, consider if the scale of the items are all working together. Decorating math tells us one large item is greater than five smalls. ■

40

Hate the sofa, hate the space

I REALLY TRIED to avoid including this rule because I wish it weren't true, but it's my responsibility to be honest. Over the twenty-nine years and fifteen different houses that I've been creating a home, I've found the one thing that makes or breaks how I feel about a family or living room is my relationship with the sofa.

When I detest looking at and sitting on my sofa, no amount of cute tchotchkes or wall art, pretty rugs or lighting can make up for the hate my heart holds for a sofa that isn't serving our family in both form and function. I wish this was something we could get past and I had a trick to make you love any sofa. I promise I've tried. But I don't. Committing to use a sofa you hate for the long haul is like forcing yourself to wear the worst pair of jeans you've ever tried on. Indefinitely. You will feel lousy every day, and everything you pair with it will be tainted.

This goes for the most prominent piece in every room. Hate your bed and you won't love your bedroom. Hate your dining table and . . . well, you get the idea.

If you don't love your sofa and are ready to make changes in the room where your sofa lives, I want to encourage you that if you do nothing else than find a way to get a sofa you love, your entire room will feel better. It's the single most impactful decision you can make. When you hate your sofa, you'll hate your space. When you hate your space, you won't fully use it, and that's a waste.

Maybe you feel that if your family says the sofa is comfortable, then you aren't allowed to change it. But comfort is only half of what a sofa provides, because even when you aren't sitting on it, you see it. If you've trained your family to think a sofa should be as comfortable and nappable as a bed and should include cupholders and remote-controlled recliners, you'll have some work to do to reintroduce a sofa that does the main job well: allow people to simply sit comfortably. It's possible to find a comfy sofa that looks great. I know you're up for the challenge.

The feeling you have about a room is directly related to how you feel about the largest piece in the room. I don't make up the rules, I just call them like I see them. ■

Pair famous couples in design

GOOD DESIGN is about relationships. Everything in your room is in a relationship with everything else, and some items naturally need and want to be paired with other items.

Here's an extreme example: your dining room table and chairs. The table can be used without chairs, I guess, but the chairs complete the table's function. How about a candlestick and a candle? Yes, there are rare occasions when you might use one without the other, but paired together they make more sense.

It's the same with other pieces. Most of the time the individual partners complete a function, but we simply don't realize how that function multiplies when they are paired together. Here are some famous couples in design to consider including in your home:

- Chair in the corner with an ottoman
- Floating sofa (in the middle of the room, not in the actual air) with a sofa table
- Sofa against a wall (not actually touching, though) with a pair of side tables
- Bed with a pair of matching nightstands
- Pair of matching nightstands with a pair of matching lamps
- Plants and containers
- Floating chair and a floor lamp
- Chandelier centered over a table
- Pair of twin lamps on a sideboard
- Pair of twin chairs in a family room
- Pair of twin chairs at the ends of a dining table ▪

42

Use skirts and show some leg

THERE ARE SOME DETAILS in design that are so subtle, you don't notice them unless you intentionally look for them. If you are making changes in a room and something about it doesn't feel quite right, check your legs and skirts.

In an ideal world, especially in a space with lots of seating and surfaces like a family room or living room, it's nice to have a mix of what is hitting the actual floor. If every piece of furniture in a room is on four-inch legs, it can leave us with a sense of uneasiness that is hard to pinpoint. This is the power of design. Most of us naturally end up with a room where there's a mix of pieces with naked legs of some sort that pick them up off the floor visually and pieces that are skirted or simply have the illusion of coming up out of the floor like a mushroom.

The mix can happen with seating, surfaces, and even storage. If your sofa and chairs are all on legs or feet, no worries. Consider your storage pieces or coffee table, an ottoman or stool, or a side table or built-in. You simply want to make sure a few pieces feel grounded to the floor to help the room feel stabilized.

The last thing I purchased for our family room was the white faceted side table. Because we already had two sofas, two chairs, and a coffee table showing some leg, I knew I wanted to add a side table that looked more grounded. Now the room feels settled. If the new white table, white swivel chair, and that wood cabinet in the back were all on legs, it simply wouldn't feel as balanced. ∎

43

Count every chair and prioritize tushies

IF OPENING UP your home and using it to host others is important to you, one helpful thing to keep in mind is to always be aware of how much seating your public rooms offer. When I was younger I would play a game with myself to see how much seating I could squeeze into a room without having it look like a chair store. (I never said I was the life of the party . . . although I could host that party.)

Look around your main hangout room right now and count how many possible places there are to sit. Our family room has nine comfy seats that permanently live there, with space to pull in extra seating if needed. That's enough for us. How do I know?

The goal is to have cushy seating for every person who lives in your home. Right now we have five people living in our home and there is a comfy seat for everyone—that's our priority seating.

You also want enough decent, comfortable seating for the number of people you find in your home on the regular. I call this secondary seating. Secondary seating doesn't need to be the most comfortable, but it also shouldn't be a backless stool pulled in from your kitchen island. It should be something where a person can sit and visit with you for an hour without needing to book a massage afterward. We regularly have the boys' girlfriends or another couple or my sister's family over, so having enough seating for us all without moving chairs into the room is my goal.

Lastly, for when you're hosting a big group, it's important to have emergency seating you can pull in so people at least have a place to sit. We have chairs on casters in our breakfast area, and our whole family knows it's easy to pull those in if we need extra seats. They are also aware of any **incognito seatos** (#44).

As you make decisions in your home, consider how many people need to sit in each room on a regular and not-so-regular basis, and let that guide you. For priority seating I'm willing to pay more and I'm a pickier shopper, wanting to actually sit in the seat before I purchase it. I'm demanding when it comes to what priority seating needs to do for me. The pieces must be beautiful *and* super comfortable. But for secondary seating I'm not as picky, and I don't mind ordering online or choosing the pretty chair over the most comfortable one. ■

44

Incognito seato

I CANNOT REPEAT this rule to myself without feeling like Adam Sandler, but isn't that the point? Now we will never forget it.

When you **prioritize tushies** (#43), you'll begin looking for ways to sneak seating into your home for seating emergencies. This is incognito seato, and it's not the extra metal folding chairs your grandmother keeps in the basement and that she's been meaning to return to the church fellowship hall for years. Not that there's anything wrong with folding chairs, but it's more fun to find creative ways to add undercover seating to your home if possible.

One of my favorite ways to add extra seating is to sneak a pair of ottoman-style stools underneath any sort of open table surface against a wall. A cube, garden stool, or pair of X-base benches work well—anything that can instantly be pulled out and into an adjoining room if needed. If you have open space in front of a fireplace, especially one with a raised hearth, consider adding an upholstered bench that can serve double duty as a surface and as emergency seating.

All our past houses have featured some sort of statement chair that doubled as a surface and could be moved around. Currently it's a metal chair sitting in a corner. Most of the time it holds a potted plant, but when we are hosting an extra-large group, the plant goes on the floor or table and the chair gets pulled to wherever we need it. Our last house had just a little bit of wall space right when you entered where we placed a chair. Guests would often put their purse on it instead of on the table right next to it. But that chair's purpose was twofold: when extra people came, it was also super lightweight and could easily be lifted with one hand and pulled into the family room.

I liked that idea so much that I looked for a chair to use the same way in our current foyer. Not once has anyone actually sat in that chair while it's in the foyer because its purpose is to be lightweight and available to move to any room of the house. When it's not in use, it just sits there waiting and looking gorgeous.

If you wish you had extra seating, don't rule out storing an extra chair or two in another room or in a place where no one will actually sit. You'll know its true purpose. ■

How big is your chest?

WE HAVE A TWIN PAIR of dressers on either side of our bed. They are pretending to be nightstands, and I admit they're large for nightstands, but I tried smaller pieces and they were too minuscule in our large room. The scale of these dressers feels nice and generous, but the drawers themselves are surprisingly, shockingly, sadly shallow.

Before I purchased the nightstand dressers, I told myself I would store the extra sheets and pillowcases in the one on my side. Once the dressers were delivered and I saw how not deep the drawers were, I realized my bed linens wouldn't all fit and tried to go back on my word, but I didn't have much of a choice.

Dana K. White, an organizing and decluttering expert, invented what she calls "the Container Concept." The Container Concept simply says that containers are actually limits. Their job is to contain and provide a stopping point. This is why chest size, drawer size, closet size, shelf size, garage size, kitchen size, and house size are important to think about.

My sheet and pillowcase container is smaller than I imagined, so I have some choices. Option 1 would be to get a bigger sheet-container dresser. However, the bigger dresser would still need to fit in the space next to my bed in my room, which in and of itself is a container with set limits. Option 2 would be to add a second container to hold my many sheets, but that also requires space within my room container that I'm not willing to give. Option 3 would be to remove stuff from another container that I already have—a shelf in my closet, for example—and dedicate that to storing my excess sheets and pillowcases. Those are my only options unless I want to add on to my house and create a larger house container.

Containers are our **bosses** (#20), and I'm glad for it. They tell us when we have enough stuff. And when they say "enough," it doesn't usually mean the container is too little but that our stuff is too much.

I used to think the problem was my house size. I didn't realize I was choosing container sizes and actual limits when I purchased a house with a certain closet size and when I purchased the dresser to be used for a nightstand. Now as I make decisions, I more fully understand that besides just picking the prettiest dresser, I'm also choosing a container that gets to boss me on how much it holds. ■

46

Marry mismatched furniture and divorce the sets

ONE OF THE FUN THINGS about decorating is that you get to be a matchmaker. Sometimes you need two pieces to work together despite having nothing in common. Not every piece in a room has to be visually related to every other piece, but sometimes we can feel in our soul that two pieces aren't working together. When that happens, consider if you can marry the pieces and create a relationship by changing one thing about one or both of the items.

If you have a great dining room table you love but the chairs are mismatched, consider painting them all the same color. This has the greatest impact when you purposely use chairs that have visual presence. They can all be the exact same style, or you can go to the opposite extreme and use chairs with noticeably different styles. Just remember that getting four chairs that are closely related won't have the same visual wow factor.

If you want to mix styles in a way that's obvious, you have to choose items with an obvious style, and **style is found in the combinations** (#21). Consider putting the following together: a tall-back chair next to a short-back chair next to a chair with rounded edges next to a chair with a modern look next to a chair with a traditional silhouette. Painting them all the same color offers cohesiveness and makes them look like a purposeful, stylish, misfit family.

There are many ways to add a common factor with mismatched pieces. Maybe you have two pieces made from similar woods. Consider refinishing and staining them the same! Or swap out the hardware for matching handles and pulls to add a sense of sameness among differing pieces.

A pair of mismatched upholstered chairs can be brought together in a closer relationship simply by styling them the same and positioning them in a way that creates balance in a room. You can create symmetry and cohesiveness between items without having to match every aspect. Find a common thread and accentuate it with flair.

In the same way, you can also divorce married couples or separate families that have run their course. For example, if you have a bedroom set that's all one wood tone and you're tired of that look, paint the nightstands, change the hardware, add a fresh stone top, remove the mirror, or refinish the wood.

You are the boss of your house. You are the justice of the peace, the divorce attorney, and the matchmaker for your stuff. ■

I divorced the top and bottom of my hutch in our previous house. Pictured here is the bottom half. See the top half paired with the kitchen counters in House Rule 79. The entire set is happily married again in House Rule 21.

47

Paint later

THE ROAD TO MISERY is paved with two-inch paint swatches.

As a naive teen, here's how I attacked decorating my bedroom. I was excited to make changes in my space. Good for my sixteen-year-old self! I first picked out the perfect peach paint color, then found a matching peach phone. This was my own private phone—connected to the family home phone number and line, of course. It had a cord and redial button and everything! Lastly, I found a comforter set from Penney's (I grew up on a last-name basis with JCPenney) to finish off the room. This plan was great because I was a child and I worked at the mall. If my comforter didn't match, I could return it to Penney's and get another one. No big deal.

Now that we are grown-ups, we need to know better. If you pick your paint color and paint the walls, then buy a sofa, chairs, rug, drapes, lamps, and pillows to work with it . . . but you don't like how it looks together in the end? You won't want to return all those items even if you could.

What's easier is getting your sofa first—be it green, pink, or neutral—finding a rug you love that's friends with the sofa colors, choosing your drapes and lighting, and *then* looking at specific paint colors. Sherwin Williams has almost two thousand paint colors, and each color can be diluted if you want. It's much easier to find a paint color to work with a rug and sofa you already have than to shop for a sofa and rug to match a sixty-dollar can of paint available in a plethora of colors.

Half the work of making good decorating decisions is simply working in the right order. Save the paint swatches for the end of the process. ■

48

Trust the homey trinity

AFTER YEARS of helping people with their homes, and mostly after moving enough times to raise eyebrows, I've figured some things out. I've learned the closest thing to the secret of decorating.

First, let me assure you that I don't like telling people they need to buy things. Mostly because I don't like being told I need to buy something. But if you believe and implement only one thing from this entire book, let it be this: you need rugs, drapes, and additional lighting.

We all know about sofas. And beds and surfaces. Most of us have an overhead light that the builder included. We've got a grasp on placing a TV across from the sofa, stacking books on a bookshelf, and putting a plant in the middle of the coffee table. What we are abusing, misusing, and ignoring over and over and over again is the trinity of rugs, drapes, and lighting.

Almost every room of your house will benefit from these three items, which is why I call them the homey decorating trinity. Designers and decorators are always trying to find the balance between form and function, beauty and usefulness. The homey trinity is the gateway to that harmony. Rooms where rugs, drapes, and extra layers of lighting weren't considered can feel unfinished, unfriendly, and uninviting.

Rugs, drapes, and extra lighting are not required, but once you add them you realize you no longer want to live without them. Of course, some rooms truly are better off without an area rug, long drapes, or additional lights, but that's less common than you think.

This idea of the homey trinity is important, and it works best when you carefully consider the function of the three elements and make sure they are the correct scale for the space.

Need a refresher on size and scale? See **nail that scale** (#39).

To learn more about drapes, read **drapes cover the wall, not the window** (#50).

Wondering why the ceiling fan light bulb isn't enough? Go to **layer your light** (#52).

Considering a rug? Turn the page for **the floor is lava** (#49). ▪

Imagine this room without the rug, drapes, and lighting. Would it feel as finished and cozy? See more of the room in House Rule 42.

49

The floor is lava

A SURPRISING SITUATION has occurred in my life. All I ever wanted to do was be a decorator, and the job I envisioned involved me buying beautiful items and placing them into people's homes all day long. It turns out, the main part of my actual job is finding creative ways to beg you to get a bigger rug. If I were an heiress to a rug empire (I'm not) or had a family crime ring funded by Big Rug (I don't), you would question my motives. But you can trust that I honestly believe you need a bigger rug and I have nothing to gain from this.

Are there rooms that don't require a rug? Absolutely.

Does your family room or bedroom need a bigger rug? Without seeing it I would still guess yes. Even over carpet.

A rug is the great connector in your room both visually and physically. When decorating, first get your seating, surfaces, and storage placed in the room. That placement then informs what rug size you need. I try to avoid formulas and measurements whenever possible, so here's how to know if your rug is working: *pretend the floor is lava.*

In the family room, you want at least the front feet of your primary seating to be securely on the rug so you can move from seat to seat to primary surfaces without getting burned by lava. Your rug will protect you.

In the dining room, you want to be able to pull out the chairs around the table and sit down without fear that the back legs will fall off the edge of the rug into hot lava.

In the bedroom, the rug goes under the bed and should be large enough that a person on either side of the bed can wake up and easily walk around the bed without fear of stepping off the rug into the molten, boiling hot lava . . . I mean floor.

These guidelines are best practices that help us make better decisions for most rooms. Yes, there will be times when a bed is off-center, a crib is in the corner, or the floor is better without a rug. But before you decide that's your situation, seriously consider if your rug is too small—showing too much lava—and maybe that's why your room feels off. ■

The previous owner had large area rugs custom bound for the odd shaped rooms— a great investment.

50

Drapes cover the wall, not the window

TRUTHFULLY, talking about window treatments is above my pay grade. There's an entire world of brilliant window treatment specialists out there, so I'm about to mention the tiniest percentage of what a window treatment can be: drapes. Now, I believe in, use, and love shutters, blinds, shades, and all sorts of other hard and soft window treatments! But when it comes to everyday decorating, our best option is often to use drapes or pair drapes with blinds that are already installed.

Drapes are long, soft fabric panels. You can buy a pair from IKEA for forty dollars, or you can have them custom-made by a designer and pay thousands, or just about every other price point in between.

There are two types of drapes. Decorative drapes, often referred to as curtains, are just eye candy. Functional drapes have a job to do such as shading from the sunlight or providing privacy.

Decorative drapes are not intended or created to ever actually be closed over the window. If your drapes consist of one layer of fabric, they are probably meant to be deco-rative; if they were functional, they would need a second layer of lining to protect them from the sun. The entire purpose of decorative drapes is to enhance the window, the view, and the light—to not obstruct these in any way. They should be hung on a rod that is installed closer to the ceiling than to the top of the window and wide enough that the drapes can hang naturally kind of bunched together without blocking any of the view. They hang almost completely over the wall and window frame.

Functional drapes that can be closed over a window usually have white lining on the back and are there to work. Their purpose is to control light and provide privacy when needed. When these types of window treatments are on the job, they cover the window. When they aren't on the clock, they are often pulled back and cover the wall like decorative drapes. Many people use functional drapes decoratively, but you should never use decorative drapes functionally.

Often a well-meaning builder or husband will install a skinny little drapery rod one inch above the top of the window glass and, if you're lucky, a few inches outside the window trim. This does no favors for your windows. I promise if you upgrade to functional or decorative drapes that can be hung higher and wider, you'll feel like you got a window enlargement, a light booster, and the ceiling raised all for the price of buying longer drapes and reinstalling your curtain rod correctly. ■

I use our functional drapes decoratively because the shutters provide privacy and light control.

51

Don't start your art until your drapes are hung correctly

GOT DRAPES? If you've never experienced the transformation that correctly hung drapes can work on a room, then you cannot be trusted to decide they aren't a necessity. This is me in bossy big-sister mode.

I'll admit, this rule is a bit of a mouthful. I first started teaching it as a type of cheer, so picture me chanting it over and over with increasingly uncoordinated cheer-like moves and using pillows for pom poms.

The point of this entire rule is ORDER. Hang your drapes before you hang your art. Why? When your drapes are hung correctly, they redefine your wall space. Because they naturally cover wall space, NOT window space, drapes make your available wall space narrower. As a result, that wall has a new center point. If you hang your art first and center it on a wall next to a drapeless window, then cover nine inches of the wall with your drapes, your art will be off-center and appear too close to the window.

Drapes hung incorrectly are worse than no drapes. If for some reason you stumbled onto this rule without reading the previous one, go back and read about how **drapes cover the wall, not the window** (#50). Getting this right will change your entire room and home for the better. ■

15

HOUSE RULES IN ACTION: 1 Learn the rules to break the rules
7 You can't ruin something you already hate 15 It doesn't have to
be perfect to be beautiful 20 Respect your boss 23 Find your own
timeless classics 32 It doesn't have to be symmetrical to be balanced
44 Incognito seato 55 Friends, not twins 64 Contrast is queen if you
want to be seen 78 Round it off and add curves 81 Use repoofable
pillows 86 Remember the sabbath and keep it homey 90 The size of
your house doesn't dictate the size of your hospitality

You don't
have to name
your style in
order to attain
your style.

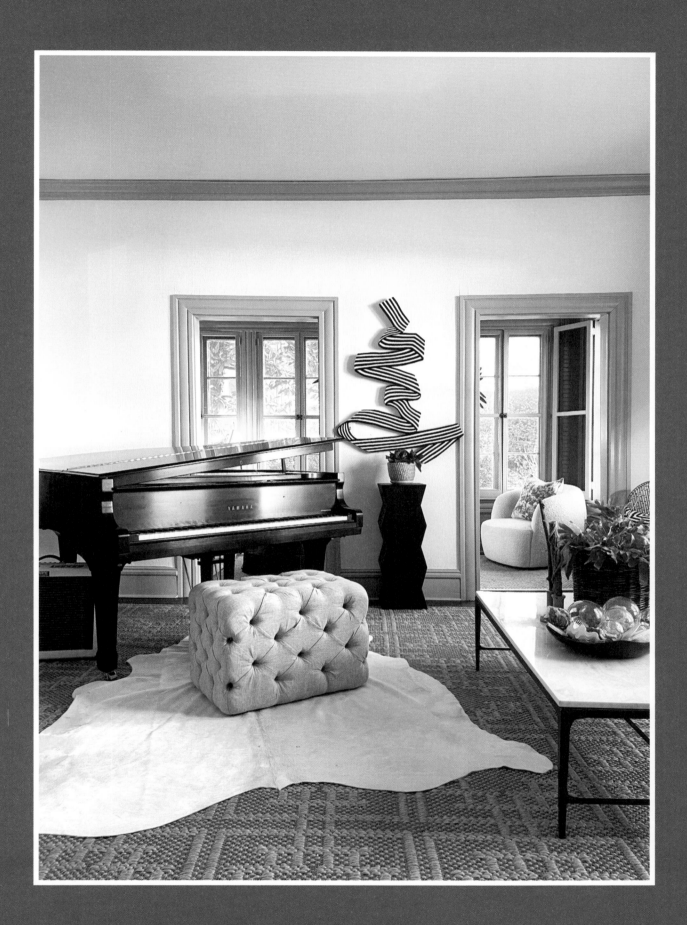

52

Layer your light

LIGHTING IN YOUR HOME is vital because it enables you to function, so it's required. Sadly, most of us are living our whole lives just squeaking by with lighting that's only adequate to see by and calling it good enough.

Have you ever looked at your laptop or phone screen and suddenly realized that the backlight was turned way down, then bumped it up? Did you experience that jolt of relief, that sense of "What have I been doing wasting my life on this dark screen?!" That's the feeling you get when you have the correct lighting in your home. It's not asking "Can I see?" but "Could this be better?" Usually the answer is yes and the change is powerful.

Let's go ahead and assume that in many rooms, the overhead light is trash. Yes, the chandelier over the table and the pendants over the kitchen island are worth their weight in gold. However, the boob light in the guest bedroom and the wimpy overhead light in the family room are not enough by themselves. It's my job to tell you that the ceiling fan in your bedroom with the light kit that sends out subtly flashing strobe lights when you turn on both functions is a menace to society and some of the worst lighting available to womankind. Do you want to look your absolute worst in your bedroom as you are getting ready every morning and as you are trying to be sexy at night? If the answer is yes, then by all means, use the ceiling fan light.

The solution is to layer in more light. I'm not telling you that you must get rid of your ceiling fan—although if you did it would look amazing to have a statement chandelier instead! I get hot at night too, and my solution is a cute little personal fan on my nightstand that I get all to myself. I do believe that whatever is on your ceiling has a hard enough time serving one purpose well; if it needs to be a fan, fine. Just add in some lamps around the room.

Lamps with shades provide a natural social media filter for our skin. They diffuse the light coming from the bulb and magically turn it into a warm, welcoming, soft glow. In general, most rooms could use at least three additional light sources besides the overhead light and windows. Don't believe me? **Shop your house** (#38) and gather three lamps and bring them all into one room and see what happens. Most likely you'll be addicted to light. ■

The floor lamp aimed over our guest book is functional, plus its dark curvy shape adds interest.

53

Let your light speak

INSTEAD OF SIMPLY LOOKING for a light you don't hate that's the right price, I want you to try to get the absolute most for your investment and look for a light with character that adds to the overall look of the room. Sometimes we forget that functional pieces can do double duty as decorative pieces, and lamps are a great opportunity to inject your personal style into a room.

I want you to **nail that scale** (#39) with your lighting. Whether it's a table lamp, floor lamp, or overhead light, most of us naturally go too small. We usually get the height right, but we wimp out on the lamp bases. When I'm shopping for lamps, I'm really shopping for lamp bases. Pretend you're looking for art or a vase or sculpture you love. Consider whether you can **combine the opposites** (#62), and if your room needs it, take this opportunity to introduce a new style factor by the shape, texture, color, and material of the lamp base.

I used to simply look for the cheapest lamps I could find that were presentable because I saw them merely as functional pieces. Now I know that **everything that sits out is a decoration** (#66), so every lamp is decor and I want to love it. My mission is not only to have the right size lamps with gorgeous shaded light but to have lamps with personality, presence, and style that add to the overall look of the room.

The same holds true for overhead lighting. Choosing overhead lighting is a balance between beauty and function. The less a light is required for an actual task, the more I aim for beauty. So my kitchen pendant lights must first be highly functional, and then I'll choose the ones I like the best. But the chandelier in our dining room just needs to add enough glowy light to eat by, so style takes the lead in that decision. ■

54

Pick the one that scares you

IT WAS JANUARY and as usual, I realized my house needed some plants. Plants and containers are a **famous couple in design** (#41). When I get a new plant I want to make sure I have the right container for it. I found a sprawling tropical plant that I loved, but it felt slightly boho for my personal style; I knew I wanted to balance it out by **combining the opposites** (#62) with a container that was a little more traditional. As I shopped, I came across a basic white glazed planter that I liked and would suit the plant just fine. But I also found a tall, oversized urn that was a little unexpected and over the top. It was also the perfect size for the plant and had a finish that would work where I needed it.

How did I decide between those two great options? I picked the one that scared me. Both options were fine, but since I wasn't choosing something like an investment sofa or wallpaper that would be a pain to remove,

I knew that the more unexpected choice had the bigger style payoff without a ton of risk.

Now, as I'm on the hunt for items in my house, I'm always looking for things I love (duh). But if something scares me a little, I want it that much more because I've learned those pieces are often what sets my personal style apart and gives the room a unique edge. This can apply to anyone's personal style. An item that scares you (and that you actually like—that's just as important) is usually a little more bossy and representative of your own style, which is a great thing. Having pieces that are unique allows you to use less to get the look you want.

The next time you're shopping for decorative pieces like art, pillows, throws, and planters and making a decision between two good, viable options, consider picking the one that's a little outside your comfort zone. If one choice feels almost intimidating—if you love it but secretly wonder what your sister will think, or if you keep walking around the store and coming back to it—this is the piece speaking to you. Start with lower-risk items and **baby-step your way** (#6) into choosing the really scary stuff—the weird, cool pieces that make your home yours. ■

55

Friends, not twins

WHEN IT COMES to choosing colors, most of the time the goal is not for colors to match perfectly but to visually go together and get along. Sadly, we'd almost rather be forced to match colors exactly because, although that seems daunting, we can know for sure whether it's a perfect match by simply heaving up our 10×14-foot wool rug that weighs 65 pounds and putting that muddy green color next to the green in the drapes. And if it's a perfect match, we're good. Easy, right?

The truth is, even if a color is an exact match, what matters is how it *looks*. Have you ever painted a room and found that one wall looks like a different color than the others just because of the light reflecting from the window? Even the same color isn't a perfect match. Instead of frustrating us, this should be freeing.

When it comes to choosing multiple types of lighting for a room, pillows to work with a rug, or pottery to use around the house, the goal is for those items to look like friends, not twins. Friends have some things in common and other things not in common, but they get along well and often complement each other's strengths.

The lighting in our family room consists of three floor lamps, two buffet-style lamps, a table lamp, and a sconce. I actually do have two sets of twins: the buffet lamps and a pair of floor/reading lamps. But beyond that, if you were to line up the various styles, you would see that together these lamps look like a cool friend group. They could be on the album cover of a band for lamps because, with the exception of the identical twins, each has its own unique personality and yet they all get along.

What they have in common are mixed metals, neutrals, and empire shades. But we've got traditional, modern, and some type of baroque style happening to make them all a bit different. If you are shopping for colors and finishes on multiple pieces—be it lamps, chairs, frames, or pillows—aim for friendship, not twinship. ▪

Twins, not friends

THE NERVE! Not only did I start a book full of rules by giving you permission to break them, but now I'm including two contradictory rules. The problem is, we're wasting time trying to perfectly match things that don't need to be matched (**friends not twins**, #55) and we aren't matching things that would make our lives so much easier if we bought them in pairs.

Every bedroom in our house was simplified once I realized that buying a pair of matching nightstands had a trickle-down effect. When you buy a pair of nightstands, it helps balance out the room. Most of the time your bed is going to be centered on a wall, and a pair of nightstands (**a famous couple in design**, #41) of equal width helps create that continued happy feeling of visual balance and well-being.

When your nightstands are twins, that means they are also the same exact height, which aids in the next step as you add lighting. Most of us enjoy having some sort of light we can turn off and on without leaving the comfort of our warm blankets, and having a lamp on a nightstand is the most popular choice. **Let it be easy** (#35): a set of twin nightstands topped with a pair of twin lamps literally cuts your decision-making in half!

If I see a lamp I love, I consider if there's anywhere I can use a second one. On a longer surface like a sofa table or dresser, a pair of lamps doubles your lighting and adds instant style. If you have a pair of side tables on either side of your sofa, a pair of lamps is a no-brainer.

Maybe you found a great chair for a great price. Can you use two? If you **prioritize tushies** (#43), tucking in a pair of chairs is a double win: more seating, less decision-making.

Even styling a sofa, bed, or front door can be easier when you aim for twins. A pair of anchor pillows in each corner of the sofa feels balanced. Twin euro pillows on the bed feels luxurious. A pair of planters with twin plants on either side of the front door feels instantly finished and welcoming.

Learning when to friend and when to twin helps simplify your decisions and your decor.

We always want a room to feel balanced, but keep in mind that **it doesn't have to be symmetrical to be balanced** (#32). Some rooms are quite symmetrical when naked, and for those I can create balance by using friends, not twins. On the other hand, some rooms are asymmetrical, and sometimes it's helpful to create symmetry and balance with twins. ▪

56

The artwork and sofa pillows show the power of friends. The nightstand dressers, lamps, and bed pillows show the power of twins. Yes, twins and friends like to hang out together in the same room!

When in doubt, carry it out

DECISION FATIGUE IS REAL, and one of the first things I look for when I'm facing a room full of decisions is the room's limitations. I want them. Not only do **limitations lead to innovations** (#3), they help narrow down our options, which can be very helpful. Decorating is about making decisions in the right order, and I'd much rather decide between ten great options than a hundred.

When we were redoing the downstairs bathroom in our current house, the options were limitless. Because this wasn't a room with furniture and rugs and drapes, I could choose whatever wall covering I wanted in any color imaginable. My only boss was the dark wood floor. I found myself paralyzed with a zillion beautiful options. So I looked at my house and let her speak into what she wanted. Were there any wall treatments that I loved already in the house?

We have a sweet little side porch that is completely covered in beadboard, even the ceiling. We have built-ins backed with beadboard in the keeping room, and it shows up again a few times in the kitchen. Decision made. Using beadboard again felt authentic to the house and added some interest to the walls. I **let it be easy** (#35) and carried an existing wall treatment farther into the home.

Our last house was on a property with a bunch of weird outbuildings consisting of random mismatched materials. I did my best not to introduce any new materials, but I took note of what was already there: white painted brick, white siding, cedar siding, flagstone in gray and cool undertones, and a green metal roof. To bring everything together as we redid the pool area and backyard, we incorporated stone coping and flagstone walkways in cool colors, added a brick wall and fireplace and painted it all white, painted the fence around the pool white, and had the brick chimney painted—you guessed it—white! I also made sure to use cool undertones in the landscaping around the house.

Repeating materials that were already in use helped make our overwhelming property feel a little more pulled together and cohesive. Plus, it made my choices so much easier. ■

58

The art of the mirror is what it reflects

WE CAN USE MIRRORS either for good or for ugly.

Sometimes a mirror may seem like a great choice for your walls. Because if you love the frame you'll love the mirror, right? Possibly.

In the last house we rented there was an awkwardly placed corner fireplace. I decided to buy a big mirror with a frame I loved to lean on the mantel. It was large enough that it filled the space without me needing to hang it. Double win!

But once I heaved it up onto the mantel and stepped back, I was appalled at what I had just done. In the center of the room hung a builder-grade fake brass, tiny pip-squeak of a chandelier that I despised. Now, with the addition of my leaning mirror, that despicable chandelier was not only in the center of my room but beautifully framed in my mirror and on display from almost every position in the room. It was as if I had added a second light fixture that I didn't like, as if I had made a photo of my most hated light, framed it, and put it on the mantel.

This was easy to remedy. Yes, I could have hung the mirror and the reflection probably would have changed just enough to place that chandelier out of frame. But something about seeing that micro chandelier in the reflection allowed me to look with fresh eyes and immediately decide that it was time to switch it out. Since we were renting, we knew we'd change it back to the original chandelier when we moved, so I put that one in a plastic bag, labeled it, and stored it in the attic. Plus, I allowed myself to purchase a great chandelier because I knew I would get to take it with me.

Now my mirror was reflecting something I loved, and it was like getting two beautiful light fixtures for the price of one.

The entire point of a mirror is *reflection*. In order to use a mirror to the fullest, make sure it's reflecting something you want to see twice. ■

59

Don't gallery-wall by accident

WE PUT THE SOFA against the biggest wall in the house as we moved in, and immediately the nine-foot ceilings created the largest opportunity I'd ever had for wall art. I was simultaneously overjoyed and overwhelmed. I decided to do what my favorite designers were doing and create a beautiful gallery wall. I did what any responsible person would do and **shopped my house** (#38), gathering up any and all possibilities for my amazing gallery wall.

Since I didn't understand the concept of **nailing that scale** (#39), I moved forward with my collection of handfuls of minuscule and microscopic wall art, assuming that if I grouped enough cute art together it would naturally look fantastic. Besides, it was all stuff I liked. What could go wrong?

Narrator: *Plenty could go wrong.*

I gave myself permission to make as many nail holes as needed to get this gallery wall right. I spent days, weeks, and even months on end adjusting the gallery wall, frustrated at why grouping a bunch of small things I liked never looked quite right. The designers made it look so easy. A gallery wall was simply a collection of beautiful pieces hung on a wall, right?

Narrator: *Wrong.*

Now I've learned that gallery walls are the highest level of wall art styling. Creating a cohesive grouping of items and hanging them in a way that's pleasing is difficult and takes intention, and 99 percent of the time you will have to purchase additional items to get the look you want.

If you are gallery-walling, keep in mind that the more items you include, the more difficult it will be to make your collection look cohesive. You want all of your pieces to feel related in a few ways—maybe frame style or color or scale or subject. Using every piece of art you can get your hands on is not a plan unless you don't care how your gallery wall looks. And we both know you care about stuff like that or you wouldn't be reading this book.

Have small items you need to show off? Placing them behind glass or displaying them on a shelf is a great way to not have to gallery-wall your lovely random teeny items. Have favorite photos or an art collection? Consider baby-stepping your way to styling art by placing your art on shelves or creating a grid formation that takes lots of options and guesswork out of the equation.

I would tell you how to create the perfect gallery wall, but it would take up the rest of this book . . . and then we'd probably still not like the way it looked. ■

60

Try the low-commitment lean

ONCE YOU LEARN to nail that scale (#39), you might find yourself with larger pieces of art than you had in the past. Congratulations! Large art is amazing, but it's also heavy and feels like a bigger deal when deciding where to put it.

One way to baby-step your way (#6) into art placement is to never hang a piece until you're sure. I know, duh. But the best way to experiment with where your art will work is to find a way to lean it against the wall you're considering. If you are placing art above a surface, find a way to set it on that surface and securely lean it against the wall as you decide if that's the right spot.

Most of the time after leaning art and liking it, I end up hanging it. But sometimes I realize I like the casual, I-can-change-it-anytime-I-feel-like-it attitude that comes with leaning art. If the art is a mirror, the reflection changes based on whether it's leaning or hung, so I'll decide which I like best.

I currently have two extra-large mirrors in our house, and both are leaners for life. Although they have hanging hardware on the back, I like better how they look when they are leaning. Plus one wall has a chair rail that is so chunky I can't hang a piece over it, so leaning was the perfect solution that added a little interest and took down the formality of the room just enough to feel like us. ■

61

Depart from sad art

I found this painting for $13 at a local thrift store. The scene was so welcoming, and when I brought it home, Chad realized it was a landscape from the county where he grew up a few hours away. A year later we moved there!

THROUGHOUT THE AGES, mothers have been handing down ancient, timeless, life-altering wisdom to their daughters about the important things that truly matter. I know my mom did. And one thing I will always remember her saying—and my sister can corroborate this—is to never hang art in your house if a scene looks so sad that you wouldn't want to be in it.

My mother did not want us to make the mistake of buying a painting of a ship approaching a stormy swell, about to be overtaken and break apart into a million pieces while the crew dies a tragic death and sinks to a watery grave. No. Don't buy that art and put it in your house, says my mother. You don't want to be transported into that art, therefore you don't want it in your house.

When it comes to choosing art for your home, sad art is bad art.

Sometimes it's not so obvious, and that's where this nugget of wisdom is helpful. If you're looking at a painting and you like it (or at least you think you like it), and the colors are right but you just aren't sure about the purchase, ask yourself if you'd want to be there. If the answer is no, you probably won't like looking at it in your house every day for the rest of your life.

I think this can even apply to abstract work if you let it. Basically, if the art feels depressing, it's a pass. You get to decide how it feels since it's going in your home. Maybe you do want to be on a ship in a storm in the middle of an ocean, and if so, now you know.

- 145 -

62

Combine the opposites

YOU DON'T HAVE to name your style in order to attain your style. However, there are some shortcuts to injecting your personal style with a punch of interest and a wow factor. One way I do this is by combining opposites.

Concepts that combine opposites are often compelling and welcoming, whether it's The Lazy Genius brand, Emily Henderson's personal style of Elevated Prairie, or my own method of Cozy Minimalism. It's a way to pull the good parts out of two seemingly opposing ideas. When done well, it's highly approachable and instantly understood.

The same goes for your style. One way to create balance, especially if you have some bossy pieces, is to combine the opposites in your home.

Combining opposites takes a previous house rule that says **style is found in the combinations** (#21) and pushes it even further to mix items that are visually different and purposely have opposing styles. This makes for interesting spaces with a sense of balance and comes in especially handy for anyone living in a house with a style that's particularly bossy and in-your-face.

Maybe you live in a rustic cabin but don't want to feel like you live in a Cracker Barrel restaurant. Easy. Just recognize your Cracker Barrel–esque house and make sure to add some pieces you love from what could feel like the opposite style to balance out the rusticness. Incorporating some shiny, slick, modern, reflective, and light-colored pieces could feel like the opposite of a rustic, primitive setting and create a pleasing visual balance.

In our living room where there is a wall full of dark built-ins, I purposely added some light pieces with the chairs, rug, drapes, and coffee table. I also appreciate the way my girly English roll-arm sofas mix and mingle with the more masculine dark wood tones and squared-off arms of our chairs. We've got a bunch of opposite textures happening as well, mixing shiny metals and natural rugs with leather, linen, velvet, vintage stained marble, and painted-over wallpaper on plaster walls. It's that push and pull that keeps the room balanced and interesting.

If you have trouble figuring out your personal style opposites, sit in a room and try to describe some items with adjectives such as matte or shiny, masculine or feminine, sharp or rounded, translucent or opaque, textured or smooth, old or new, dark or light, large-scale or small-scale, detailed or simple. Whatever you have lots of, be sure to add in some of its opposite to balance out the space. ■

Our living room features a masculine, squared-off leather cigar sofa paired with rounded boucle chairs and a baroque-style table with lots of carved detailing that I painted with black chalk paint.

63

Disrupt the timeline

IF YOU READ any shelter magazines or watch HGTV, you've probably heard a designer mention a look that is **collected over time** (#88). It's a feeling of a home that doesn't look like someone went and purchased everything in their room as a set on the exact same day from the exact same store. Ideally, you want some items in your home to look like they had a history and have been passed down for generations, representing different tastes, eras, and origins. Mixing pieces of different ages and styles gives a home a sense of place and a soul.

If your home was born with style and has an obvious or bossy heritage like a Crafts-man bungalow or a historic log cabin or a mid-century modern—congratulations! You already have one era represented. If your home wasn't born with style, no problem. You're going to get to mix eras with your stuff.

The Victorian foyer has a touch of California Casual mixed with a bit of British Isles flair.

My Queen Anne Victorian house allows me to introduce some obviously non-Victorian pieces by considering what eras aren't represented. Pieces that represent styles such as art deco, modern, traditional French country, English farmhouse, Spanish—heck, even brutalism—are up for grabs to be purposely mixed and matched. This creates a home that's full of interest and quiet (or loud) unexpected pieces.

Just because you live in a farmhouse in the country doesn't mean everything in your house must be farmhouse inspired. It's actually the opposite. This is an opportunity to mix pieces from other styles you admire. It's just like **combining the opposites** (#62), but this time you're using eras and styles instead of adjectives.

If your home is feeling one-note, or if you are looking to buy a piece of furniture and aren't sure where to begin, look around and pay attention to what recognizable styles are represented that can be traced back to a specific era. Then consider what other styles you enjoy and if you can work some pieces into your home from those eras, since **style is found in the combinations** (#21). Your home will be more well-rounded and more soulful for it. ▪

64

Contrast is queen if you want to be seen

SOMEONE ONCE ASKED how I would decorate with and feature a large basket made completely out of thin black wire. I told them I wouldn't try to feature something like that because I try not to decorate with invisible things. Up close, a wire basket is interesting. From a few feet away, it begins to look like nothing, and in a room it completely disappears.

Think about it. If you are purposely adding beauty and function to a room, nine times out of ten you want the items you are using to actually be seen and have visual impact. This is why, if you have a huge two-story room where the walls and ceiling are painted white, adding a big white chandelier, white mirror, and white furniture might not be the best use of your money because they will disappear against the white walls and ceiling. They become invisible.

Lucky for us, the opposite happens too. Have a dark two-story room? A white chandelier and light-colored furniture will pop against that.

For that white room, try adding darker pieces. Contrast allows things to get the attention they deserve and brings items you want to be noticed to the forefront.

There are times when you actually don't want to see something, like when you have a piece that you don't love but have to use anyway. Let's say you have a dresser that isn't your favorite. To make it fade into the background, consider painting it the same color as the wall.

Incorporating high contrast allows items to be seen, and lower contrast allows items to blend together. This is not good or bad; it's just helpful, neutral information. So the next time you're choosing a pillow or wall art or fabric for your drapes, ask yourself if you want it to actually be seen or to disappear into the background. ■

65

Subtle but significant

AFTER A FEW MINUTES on Instagram or Pinterest, it's easy to believe that in order to make any sort of impact in your home you've got to make some huge, remarkable, swooping changes. One of the things that gets lost in the shuffle of small online images is details.

I believe there are three types of people: those who need big patterns, color, and boldness in their homes, those who crave utter simplicity, and those of us in the middle who prefer a little quiet drama.

Quiet drama is difficult to capture but easy to experience. It's texture, attention to detail, a change of a sheen of paint. If you like some subtle interest, you are the kind of person who enjoys the delight of little details in your home. Don't discount those.

I felt a tiny bit foolish when making decisions for our current downstairs bathroom. We needed to redo the walls, ceiling, lighting, trim, and even the sink. Everything was an option to create a big statement. I chose to cover the walls in beadboard because **when in doubt, carry it out** (#57), and we added some extra molding around the baseboard and crown to cover gaps and add interest. Much to no one's surprise, I had the walls painted in my go-to Sherwin Williams Extra White and the trim painted in a quiet contrast of Sherwin Williams Gossamer Veil. It's not showy, so it sometimes feels like I'm taking the easy or safe way out, but I know I'm not. There's a lot happening in this room if you just take a moment to notice. What else does someone have to do as they sit on the toilet?

Creating margin and literal, visual white space in a room can be just as purposeful and impactful as those big signature pieces. The goal is to find your unique and perfect balance for your personal style. ■

66

If it sits out, it's a decoration

SOMETIMES I'LL WALK through my house and suddenly realize there's a bunch of stuff sitting out, having a visual impact on my home in a way that I never intended. I've become blind to it all because it's been there for so long.

Next to the kitchen sink there's an assaulting color of dish liquid packed in a glaring little advertisement next to brightly colored sponges and dish towels that look like they've been picked out by someone who's never even met me. The box of donations by the back door has been collecting dust for weeks, and the Kleenex box is demanding attention with its obnoxious pattern. I've spent all this time and effort creating a cohesive, visually beautiful home, but there are a bunch of functional items sitting out and having a say on the overall look and feel of it.

The truth is, everything that sits out in your home is a decoration.

Whether we admit it or not, when an item is out on display, we are decorating with it, and it either enhances or takes away from the overall experience.

If I'm going to have tissues sitting out in my family room 365 days a year, I want to make mine pretty, so I'll look for pretty covers that work with my style. If soaps and scrubbers that I look at and use multiple times a day are front and center in my kitchen, well then, make mine pretty. Let's elevate that experience. Guess what? It doesn't cost more to buy a pretty dishrag versus one in a crazy color.

I'm more apt to declutter if I have a place near the back door dedicated for donations. Great! But instead of living the rest of my life with a ripped Amazon box as floor decor that I look at twenty-seven times a day, I can pay attention to the fact that I need something to function there instead. I choose to believe it's worth it to upgrade the visual experience. So I'll find a pretty lidded basket for my donation station.

I LOVE this part of creating a beautiful, functional home. I've also learned that when I upgrade those functional items to prettier options, they serve as decor. And surprisingly, my house needs less stuff!

Because everything that sits out in your home is technically a decoration, invest in pretty everyday items that don't fight against or clash with your existing decor. If you have to look at it, why not make it beautiful *and* functional? If it sits out, make it stand out. ▪

FINISH WHAT YOU STARTED

I MIGHT BE the world's worst finisher. I'm a proud imperfectionist, and tragically, I realized early on that finishing something in my home to 80 percent gave me great joy and looked a lot better than when I started. So off I went to the next shiny and fun project. I had drapes that needed to be hemmed and steamed, empty containers ready to hold my plants that needed repotting, and half-painted pieces of furniture. (I actually still have that one.)

The truth is, there was a time in my life while I was actively raising three little boys when good enough was truly better than done, and that concept served us well. But I collected some bad habits and forgot about the satisfaction that comes with actually finishing a project.

If you are a chronic non-finisher, make it a goal to finish something. I like to start with something visual so I can personally enjoy the last little percentage even though I know most people will never notice. Finishing projects to completion has helped me feel more grown-up and responsible and gives me a sense of accomplishment that feels as good as making something simply look better.

The rules in this section are for both finishers and non-finishers. But they'll mostly apply to projects and spaces that are closer to being done than just getting started. If you've already made a lot of decisions in a room and can't figure out what looks off or why you don't love everything together even though you love the individual items, these tips can help you finish off a space.

Stored away or on display

YEARS AGO, while I was on my annual climb to the attic to get our Christmas decorations, I came across a couple boxes of meaningful mementos carefully packed away and safely hidden from humanity for the ages. There were old family photos of my grandfather's barbershop quartet, some timeless kitchen items I remembered my grandmother using, and even professional photos of our boys I had printed on quality paper but never took the final step to actually frame and display.

I brought the boxes down, but when I looked around my house I realized I didn't have room to display any of those special items.

The few open shelves in my kitchen were dedicated to pure function and held an old toaster, a blender I rarely used, and a KitchenAid mixer that I used from time to time. Our limited surfaces held items like the decorative box of mail I needed to go through, another cute box for my massive coupon clipping binder (yes, I was that person), and yet another decorative box full of school papers I needed to sort.

But in looking through the pile of meaningful beauty from the attic, I realized that I didn't want to pack it back up. It seemed wrong to display my kitchen tools as if they were the crown jewels of our family—especially the ones I never or rarely used—while storing pieces that deserved to be on display. I was doing it backwards by displaying items that could be stored and storing items I wanted to display.

I ended up making room in our pantry to store the blender and toaster, simply moving them to the counter temporarily when we used them, so that I had room to display a few heirloom pieces in the kitchen next to my mixer.

I decided that even though the mail, coupons, and school papers were important and used weekly, I didn't have to set them out on display in order to use them—especially when that meant some of my favorite, more meaningful and beautiful mementos were crowded out and not appreciated or enjoyed.

Now I keep myself in check by looking at my counters and shelves and making sure I'm displaying display pieces and storing what needs to be stored. Besides, if **everything that sits out is a decoration** (#66), I don't want to be decorating my house with pieces that could easily be stored behind a door or in a drawer, still within reach. For something meaningful, honor and enjoy it by using it, not storing it. ■

68

Cluster your collections

IF YOU'VE EVER READ a book about decluttering, many of the experts will tell you the best way to make good decisions about whether to keep items or get rid of them is to gather everything you have in that category and then evaluate. If you don't see it all together, you don't truly know what you have. Decluttering sweaters? Gather all your sweaters together, then keep what you have room for. Decluttering pens? Same.

In some weird way, I think this also applies to decorating and displaying collections. The best way to enjoy your collections and let them have maximum impact is to group them together and display a collection in your house as one.

I love black-and-white and brown-and-white transferware. At first I kept my collection of dishes stacked in a cabinet. Then I realized I didn't want them **stored away but on display** (#67), so I decided to find a way to display the bowls and plates. I could have sprinkled them around the house—a bowl here by the back door to hold the keys, a plate there under a plant, a saucer hung over a piece of art—but instead I chose to cluster my collection.

Hanging my hodgepodge, motley crew of random, secondhand transferware all together on the same wall suddenly gave it much more meaning, impact, and presence than I imagined. My collection of plates and bowls was finally getting the attention it deserved because together these little mismatched items were seen as one. Not only did it look great, but it gave my collection a place of importance in our home.

A side perk: once I had my wall the way I wanted, I had a stopping point and no longer needed to collect every cute piece of neutral transferware I came across. My collection feels complete. ■

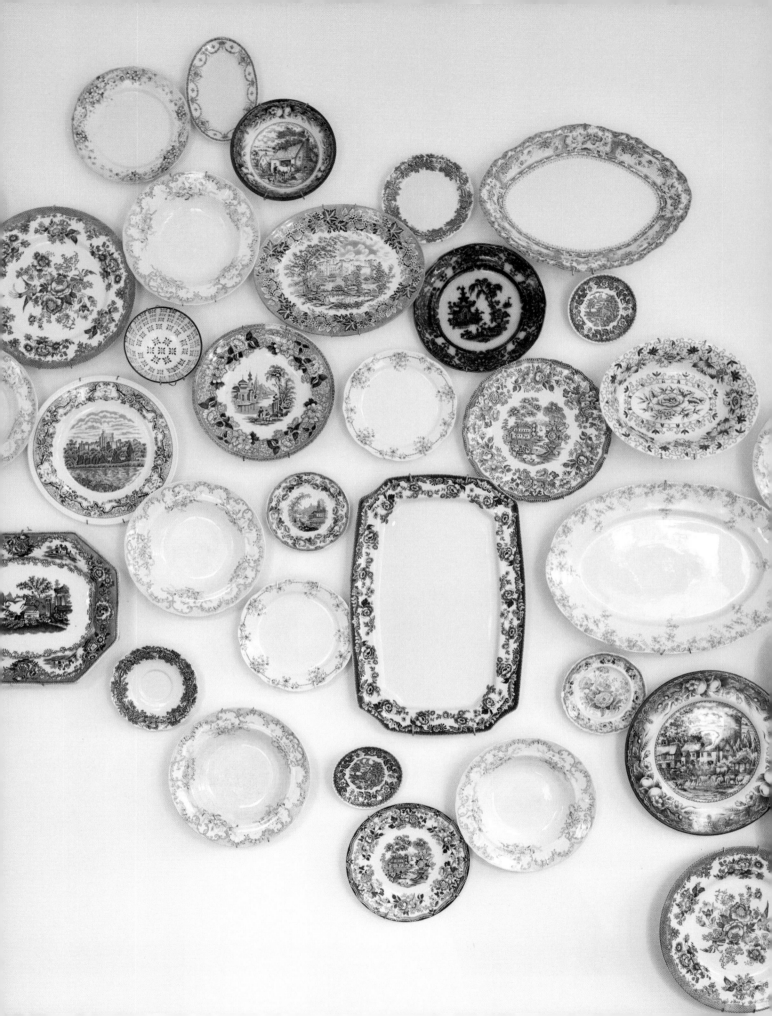

69

The rule of pineapple

LIVING IN FIFTEEN different houses as an adult (so far) means I've experienced setting up house and all the fun and frustration that comes with moving multiple times. As much as I sometimes hated packing up and unpacking yet again, it was part of a great education in all things home. I do believe that one of the best ways to learn is by making a mistake and then figuring out what went wrong so you never have to make it again. I've made lots of mistakes, but the best part about me is that I paid attention and learned from them.

In every house I would look forward to the day that I had unpacked enough to get to do some styling. Decorating a new mantel or creating a pretty vignette on a surface for the first time is still my favorite part of moving. There were usually some decorating gaps, and being the frugal, responsible woman that I was, I'd run off to HomeGoods looking for something. Anything. The less expensive, the better.

Aimlessly shopping for "something" is asking for trouble. My dedication to spending less was admirable but often resulted in poor decision-making because I didn't realize that **just because something costs less doesn't mean I'm saving money** (#33). I usually arrived home with a handful of tiny items. Larger items cost more, so I was smart and went small.

Sadly, these tiny trinkets and micro decor pieces didn't make much of an impact when placed on our mantel. Naturally, I assumed that meant I needed even more tiny trinkets to fill the space. You know where this is going.

I had to learn that if I want to make a visual impact in a room, especially if I'm going out shopping for something to style a vignette, I need to always look for something more substantial and **nail that scale** (#39). So I made up a rule that I could only purchase items larger than a pineapple.

This doesn't mean I don't have things smaller than a pineapple—I do. And from time to time I might buy something small, like a little inlaid box or a bud vase, which is fine as long as I'm not intending those to make a difference with their presence.

Shopping for decor? Remember the rule of pineapple. ■

70

Layers invite

IN HIS BOOK *The Beauty Chasers*, Tim Willard tells the story of painting an image of the woods with his daughters. He tells of how, after using red paint and then covering over it with another more "foresty" color, some of the red paint was exposed beneath. The surprising layering effect created the look of light shining into a deep forest. It was hard to look away from the image it created.

He writes that he shouldn't have been surprised, because he already knew that "layers invite."

Did you know that layers invite? Because I never realized that truth until I read it in Tim's book about beauty. Now I repeat it to myself two or three times a week. And as usual, because I wear house-colored glasses, I must instantly apply everything to home. Here goes.

Layers of quilts and fluffy down comforters on a bed *invite you to rest*.

Layers as you look down a hallway through multiple rooms *invite you to wander through*.

Layers as you pull up a long driveway and start to glimpse the home through the trees pique your interest and *invite your curiosity to come closer*.

A sunset of one color is nice. A sunset with layers of red, orange, and cotton-candy pink is captivating, an invitation to linger.

Whether it's in art, nature, or our homes, layering leads to interest, captures our attention, and invites us to experience a moment more fully.

Have you ever seen a photo of a living room where the only furniture is seating and it's all lined up flat against the walls? It's so uninviting. Something as simple as layering a coffee table in the center, layering a pair of chairs in front of the fireplace, or layering a rug over a wood floor makes all the difference. Layering is an artist's trick that creates an invitation. ◼

71

Get your greens

IF YOU SPEND TIME online scrolling through home hashtags on social media or perusing home interiors on Pinterest, I encourage you to pay attention to the plants, trees, and flowers you see. They are everywhere. You will start to feel like plants are taking over the world. It kills me to be this cliché, but without plants a room feels lifeless.

Here's some good news. Besides **plant math** (#72), there are ways to cheat the system a little and still have the look of plants without the remembering-to-water-them part. The trick is to focus on greens instead of only potted plants. Greens are anything that adds some alive-looking plants to your home. Adding live plants to your home isn't required (although I'd like for it to be), but adding greens absolutely is.

The easiest, lowest commitment level for adding greens is cutting stuff out of your own backyard—or your mom's yard or your neighbor's yard—and bringing it into your house. Whenever I mention this, people come to me suddenly worried about bugs. Fine. You can worry about bugs and ask me about them,

as long as you also ask every gardener who cuts roses and brings them inside. There is a double standard and clearly I have feelings about this. If bug worries plague you, simply shake or spray off anything you cut from the yard before you bring it inside.

By cutting branches from your yard, you are **baby-stepping your way** (#6) into convincing yourself to get an actual plant. Bringing free yard greens inside will have an astonishing impact, and you will become addicted to fresh greens. Grab some garden shears and cut your branches twice as long as you think you'll need. Bring in your yard cuttings, pair them with a big funky vase, and finally understand why plants are taking over the world.

Greens can also come in the form of grocery store flowers or flowers cut from your garden. There are even some fantastic preserved greens; I have some preserved asparagus fern that looks amazing.

Greens can be pretend plants, but if you must do this, find the most realistic looking plants possible. Fake greens should look so good that everyone will assume they're real. Choose the higher quality pretend plant, put it in a better pot, add real soil, and fool us all. ▪

Page through this book and notice all the greens in the photos. How would the rooms feel if they were missing?

72

Plant math

YOUR PLANT will die one day.

Maybe in two months. Maybe in two years. Maybe in two decades. But that's no excuse for not buying and learning to care for a plant. Yes, there are some fantastic faux plants, and if you like those, you should use them. But too many people pass on real plants because they are afraid they can't keep them alive. The purpose of a live plant isn't immortality. Live plants clean the air, are rewarding to keep, and have a unique beauty. It's worth it to find a plant or two you love.

If you pay twelve dollars for a plant and it lives six months, you're paying two dollars a month to enjoy that plant. That's 6.7 cents a day to have a beautiful green plant in your home. And that's only if it dies after six months. What if it lives for years?

Most of us are willing to spend six dollars on a bundle of grocery store flowers that will die after a week, but spending twice that amount on a living plant that I promise will live more than twice that long feels like a risk.

The more you practice caring for plants, the quicker you'll find the type of plant that you can easily keep alive. It's kind of like finding your plant soulmate. We each have a level of care we're willing to give, we have different amounts of light available and different humidity levels in our homes, and some plants will naturally be happier with us than others. Enjoy the experience of finding your plant soulmate.

Consider picking up a plant the next time you're at the supermarket or home improvement store, or stop by your local nursery. Before you go, keep an eye on the places in your house that could use some green and notice if they get actual sunbeams, filtered light, or hardly any natural light. When you're in the store looking at plants, read the tags to see what kind of light each one needs and choose accordingly.

As Emily P. Freeman says, "Pick what you like, then see how it grows." ■

73

It doesn't have to be living to add life

YOU NEED GREENS in your life, and as much as I believe this, there are other ways to add a sense of the natural world to your home without having to keep something alive.

In the past five years, our family has been lucky enough to visit both Yellowstone and Yosemite National Parks. Both parks are in a part of the country that feels completely opposite to where we live and the natural world that we've been exposed to. So when we came across rock and mineral stores, we thought that purchasing some fascinating specimens could be a fun way to remember our trip. Along the way we also picked up a few pieces of nature (not from the parks themselves): A stone from the yard at the Airbnb where we stayed. A pine cone off the grounds of the campsite near another cabin. A piece of petrified wood the guide handed my son as they fly-fished one afternoon.

When we got home I gathered all the bits and pieces and store-bought rocks onto a **home base** (#74), and it's one of our family's favorite ways to remember the trip. Now I look for natural bits and baubles everywhere we go. An annual trip with friends to the beach is remembered by shells, stones, and sea glass stored in a shell box I bought from one of those touristy shops. When my boys take a trip, they often bring back a rock or a feather or something else to remember the place by.

Besides rocks, feathers, and shells, here are some other ways to add a bit of nature to your home:

- pelts and furs (we have some as arm protectors on our chairs)
- vintage turtle shells
- hide and sheepskin rugs
- items made of natural materials: raw wood or live-edge pieces, clay pottery, and natural stone
- natural fabrics like wool, linen, cotton, jute, silk, and leather
- incorporating fire: fireplace, candles, tabletop fire pit
- opening windows and doors
- yard cuttings brought indoors

Layering in a few natural items helps a place feel less sterile. Your home should feel like the opposite of an operating room. ▪

74

Aim for home base

BECAUSE I WANT the most amount of style with the least amount of stuff, being purposeful with every item on display is important to me. Plus, we all know that **if it sits out, it's a decoration** (#66) whether we intend to decorate with it or not. That can create a bit of a dilemma in high-functioning areas like the bathroom, the kitchen, and the table by the back door.

Sometimes we need a bunch of little functional items at our fingertips. In the kitchen near the stove I want the salt, pepper, and wooden spoons. Next to the sink I need the soap, a scrubber, and maybe a candle. On the nightstand I want to have a glass of water, my hand lotion, ChapStick, and emergency Tums. These areas are all opportunities to create a sweet little family, and you do that by providing them with a home base.

A home base is a decorative drop zone with limits that gathers all the items you need in a beautiful way so that they are still functional. Instead of seeing eight individual items sitting on a surface, a home base visually turns them into one. It's decorating magic! A home base can be a tray, platter, shallow basket, slab of stone, wooden box, large hardbound book . . . you get the idea.

Any time you need a few functional items to sit out together, consider if a home base could help. I have one to contain our keys, coins, sunglasses, and such on the surface at the back door. You could have one on the coffee table for reading glasses, remotes, and coasters. I want my home base to be gorgeous just as I want everything *in* the home base, those functional things I use on the regular, to look beautiful too. ■

75

Surfaces declare their purposes

FOR YEARS I assumed every surface in our home was my personal playground and a place to display my unique style. I would fiddle and fret and change up each surface until I had it just right.

The dining room table had a grouping of pretty vases.

The hearth was filled with baskets that were filled with dusty pillows.

The coffee table was covered to within an inch of its life with a curated collection of stacked books, a plant, cute seasonal tchotchkes, and a few favorite candles.

My house had absolutely ZERO breathing room, and to do anything from starting a puzzle to folding laundry, working on homework, or setting the table for dinner required first moving pretty things out of the way (to where? every other surface was full) to create some space on a surface so we could use it.

My surfaces were telling on me. They were announcing to the world that their sole job was to look pretty. And that's true for some surfaces some of the time. But I was insisting that all surfaces look pretty all of the time. Without realizing it, I was forcing us to live our lives in service to the vignettes I had created.

I was worried I couldn't get my cozy style without completely filling up my house and surfaces with pretty things. I'm not saying it was ugly or wrong—although it was trouble. I'm saying there's another way.

If **our home exists to serve us** (#4), then our surfaces are also part of that. I learned it's actually acceptable and helpful and surprisingly beautiful to have some surfaces in my home left undecorated, unstyled, quiet, and empty. These dedicated empty surfaces are an invitation to do the stuff of life without first having to clear them off. ■

76

Let your refrigerator run around naked

IF YOU NEED to uncomplicate your home a bit and only have four minutes, try clearing off the fridge. All. The. Way.

Enter any appointment reminders into a calendar, pack away that magnet-hung art you want to keep, save the photos you love, and toss the rest. A few houses ago our washer and dryer were in a mudroom, but the sides of the machines were exposed. So that's where we chose to put magnets and reminders. That way we weren't faced with them every time we needed milk. Our refrigerator has been naked ever since, and we're never going back.

The longer you've lived with a visually loud refrigerator, the bigger the impact it will have on your life to let it go naked for a while. Plus, it's a sneaky way to trick yourself into wanting to clean off more things. I'm always looking for simple ways to get big wins, and the naked fridge will have your family asking why the kitchen feels bigger, emptier, tidier, and why you look so young and fresh.

Undressing your fridge allows you to **baby-step your way** (#6) to quiet your kitchen and have a micro moment of visual margin in your daily life. ■

77

Rainbowetical order

THERE ARE TIMES we need to have lots of random stuff on display either out in the open or right behind a closed door. Maybe you have a pantry, home library, homeschool room, or simply a closet that is visually loud. Because we've come to terms with the fact that **everything that sits out is a decoration** (#66), one side effect is that we hold our stuff to a higher visual standard.

If you are the kind of person who wants to create visible order out of chaos and you are dealing with a grouping of items with a zillion different colors all mixed up, it can feel overly random. One way to bring order to lots of color chaos is to simply organize by the rainbow: ROYGBIV. Red, orange, yellow, green, blue, indigo, violet.

It's the secret to The Home Edit's success—they're simply **clustering their collections** (#68) based on color. And it can work for all sorts of things. Have an essential oil collection? ROYGBIV it. Want your closet to feel a little more put together? Simply hang your clothes in rainbowetical order. Even local thrift stores do this with their hanging clothes. They know that it creates visual order, plus if someone's looking for a red shirt they know where to find it.

One day my oldest son had his disc golf bag out and was looking at his "clubs," which if you don't know are fancy frisbees in a bunch of bright colors. He left the room and I quickly organized them in rainbowetical order, and he walked back in and loved it. That was years ago, they're still in rainbowetical order today, and my other disc-golfing son has adopted that filing system too. It looks eye-catching, plus each disc is easy to find.

If you are a highly visual person this can even work for books. For the most part, I can tell you the cover color for every book I own. If you're like that too, you'll be able to easily find books even if they are organized by color. Purists will be mad at us, but here's the truth: 99 percent of the time I own a book, I'm not reading it. It's on display. And if it's on display, it's got to contribute to how my house looks AND I want to be able to find it. Our personal libraries are there to serve us however we need them to.

Currently most of our books are in a bookcase with doors, but it brings me a little zing of joy every time I open the doors and see a rainbow looking back at me. ∎

78

Round it off and add curves

LOOK AROUND your room and notice all of the right angles happening at every corner. (Get it?) Right angles are literally built into our homes: room shape, doorways, windows, bookshelves, large case goods, framed art, rugs, fireplaces, hearths, mantels, TVs, mirrors, beds, books, frames. I could go on but I'll stop. None of us need to add right angles in our homes.

However, most of us need to be purposeful about adding curves. If a room lacks curves it feels sharp. To help soften it up, simply add some rounded edges. If you want a mirror over the dresser, try a round mirror. Need an extra lamp? How about a curvy one?

If you are styling a surface or mantel, you want to evaluate and make sure you include curves in your vignette. When I'm styling a mantel, I'll always start with a piece of art that's about two-thirds the size of the fireplace below. Usually that art has right angles, so I purposely look for a curved vase or planter to add some rounded shapes. Then I add some yard cuttings or a houseplant to introduce an organic shape.

Decorating is all about balance and relationship between the items in your home. Your signature style shows up in how you create that balance and relationship. But no matter what your style is, everyone can benefit from mixing up curves and angles. ■

THE TINY MESS

MAGNOLIA TABLE   JOANNA

Magnolia Table

COOPER & THIEF

RED WINE BLEND

2019

79

Vase your space

YOU GRAB A BOUQUET of flowers from the grocery store. When you get home, you reach for that one tall, skinny, clear glass vase you have under the sink. You cut the ends off the flower stems (because you know this trick), push them down into the vase of water, set it on the mantel, then wonder why it doesn't look like the bouquet of grocery store flowers you saw that social media influencer put on *her* mantel.

As you stand back and look at that clear vase of flowers on your mantel, 80 percent of what you see are the stems in water and the underside of some of the flowers, plus some color on top where all the blooms are smashed together and fighting for attention. Part of the problem is the placement. Maybe they should be on the coffee table so you're looking down on the flowers. But much of the problem is with that tall, skinny glass vase that is now strangling your flowers and showing off the part them that isn't very pretty: the stems.

You need vases—opaque ones, not clear, of different shapes and sizes and with different size openings. A bouquet of grocery store flowers requires a large opening. A few branches cut extra long from your favorite blooming tree will look great in a stout, sturdy vase with a medium opening. And the single gardenia your daughter picked for you calls for a vase with a small opening. Once you understand your **need for greens** (#71), vases, flowers, and cuttings will become a bigger part of your life in all the most wonderful ways.

You'll know you have a great vase when you can even use it empty. From where I'm sitting in my family room as I write this, I can see three vases. One holds preserved greens, and the other two are empty because they are pretty and interesting on their own. Your vases should be beautiful on their own, represent your personal style, and be able to add to the decor of the room even when not holding greens. No need to hide them under the sink. ■

80

Threes, please

I LOVE A HOME with mixed woods, mixed metals, and layers and layers of mixed neutrals. A question I often get asked in the classes I teach is how to successfully mix materials so that a room looks cohesive and purposeful instead of random and weird.

The answer lies in an old decorator's trick to rely on threes. Groupings of three, the rule of thirds, and the golden ratio can be traced back through the ages, but all you need to know is that if you want something to look purposeful, either group it in threes or repeat it at least three times.

If you want to mix dark and light wood in your family room, simply make sure you incorporate light wood in at least three places and dark wood in at least three places. This doesn't mean it must be a large piece of furniture. If you have dark wood floors, you only need to add dark wood in a few other places—maybe a side table and a dark wood frame around a mirror. If you are mixing this with light blond wood, maybe the coffee table, a chunky candle holder, and the mantel are all made of the same wood color. Repeating something three times makes it obvious that you are mixing on purpose and helps visually "sprinkle" the material around the room. The same holds true for metals or colors.

Threes can also guide you when styling a surface. I'm a fan of having one large statement piece like a gorgeous plant in a container on a table. But if you are creating a grouping, aim for threes. Two can look empty, four can feel odd (even though it's even!), but three items usually feels balanced. ■

Three pieces of thrifted art create a collection. Three differently patterned pillows look purposefully curated.

81

Use repoofable pillows

HAVE YOU EVER brought home a pair of pretty little pillows for your sofa, tucked them into the corners all cute like, and by the next week after your husband used them to nap on and your kids used them to help stabilize their fort, both pillows are flat and ruined? Don't blame your family, blame the pillow.

Only buy pillows that have two separate parts: the cover, which is the pretty fabric on the outside that has a zipper, and the insert, which is the fluffy stuff on the inside that is enclosed in a second layer of white fabric. That insert and the fluff inside is what makes or breaks how your pillow functions. I believe pillows are meant to be used and abused and then should be expected to fluff back up. The only way to achieve this is by using pillows with feather inserts or, if you're allergic, a good down alternative.

These days a lot of retailers carry pillows with feather inserts, but many still sell pillows stuffed with polyfill. That's the awful teddy bear stuffing that is the spawn of Satan and will never fluff back up but only get flatter and make you want to die.

When you are pillow shopping, look for pillows where the pillow cover has a zipper. That way you can remove the cover and wash it, but it also gives you access to the pillow insert. If the insert is feather stuffed, you'll know because you can flatten it, then fluff it back up right there in the aisle. If the insert is of Satan, you can still purchase the pillow as long as you are willing to change out the insert. Maybe you have an extra feather insert at home in the same size. Or you could simply buy a feather insert online.

Pro tip: for maximum fullness and fluffiness, look for an insert that is an inch or two larger than the pillow cover.

Yes, feather pillows will shed a few feathers. That's proof you did it right. I simply pull out any poky feathers and drop them on the floor, and they get picked up the next time I vacuum. You could also add a second pillow cover if your pillows are extra pokey. I switch out my pillow covers a few times a year. It's a simple way to add seasonal color and texture and doesn't take up much storage space. Keep the covers folded up in a basket and change them out whenever you feel like it.

These days, higher-end shops and Etsy artists often sell only the pillow covers themselves and assume you have invested in your own quality inserts. And now you will. ◾

82

Trendy or trending

IT WAS 2010 and the zigzag chevron pattern was on everything from tea towels to pillows, rugs, drapes, chairs, wallpaper, mugs, and clothing. Chevron moved from timeless to trending to trendy, and as it began to cover too many things, the majority of us grew tired of it. Chevron itself wasn't bad, but the application of something can feel timeless, trendy, or trending depending on how we the people handle it.

Let's loosely define the terms.

Timelessness in decor points to something that doesn't really go out of style, such as medium-brown wood floors, quiet Carrara marble, white subway tile, an English roll-arm sofa, or a brass pharmacy-style floor lamp. Most of us could add these items into our home and they would work with our personal style today, ten years ago, or twenty years from now.

Trendy is a phase. In one day, out the next. It's the "Live, Laugh, Love" signs, the black-and-white buffalo plaid on the welcome mat, the 2010 chevron on the drapes. It's usually about a specific application of something and can feel overused.

Trending is often (but not always) something timeless that's having a moment. This can get tricky because I just said black-and-white buffalo plaid on a welcome mat was trendy; however, buffalo plaid in and of itself is a bit timeless and also has its trending moments. The same goes for chevron and herringbone. They are actual timeless patterns we can trace back through history, but when applied in a certain way over and over (and over and over and over!) they can move from trending to trendy and feel dated in a bad way.

When we talk about something being trendy, it's usually a negative because that means it has passed out of popularity and feels overdone. But when we say something is trending, that simply means it's popular.

A chesterfield sofa is timeless, but it was also trending back in the 2010s. Even so, I'd take a chesterfield in my home right this moment if someone wanted to give me one.

Unlacquered brass is timeless, but it's been trending with the masses for the past few years.

Copper, silver, chrome, nickel, oil-rubbed bronze, and brass are all timeless, but they take turns trending and one is usually more popular than the others.

Heavily veined marble started trending again a few years ago. Marble is timeless, but certain styles trend in and out.

I love having fun with trends and adding a few in the form of colors, patterns, or fabrics on a throw pillow or low-commitment piece. But when it comes to investment pieces, I've learned to choose more timeless pieces, even if they are trending. ■

Commit to low-commitment color

THIS IS ONE of my personal house rules. Yes, you can **make your own house rules** (#98). There are so many options to choose from when decorating that it can quickly become overwhelming. **Limitations are lovely and needed and actually lead to innovations** (#3). So I decided to set my own limit when it comes to using color in my home.

After purchasing a teal cabinet only to end up neutralizing it with paint a few months later, I finally paid attention to how fickle I can be with color. One way I've decided to limit myself is to not use bold color on my investment and long-term pieces. This includes upholstered pieces like a bed, sofa, or chair; large case goods like tables, bookshelves, and dressers; and area rugs. When it comes to hard finishes like tile, backsplashes, counters, and floors, I purposely force myself to pass by glorious colorful options and pick a neutral. It has saved me from myself multiple times.

Here's the thing—I don't hate color. In the spring I love sweet greens and chartreuse. In the summer I want crisp blue and white . . . then immediately remember that pink, red, and orange are the happiest combination ever. Come fall I want muddy cool colors and rusty warm colors. And in the winter I've got to have texture and sparkle, darks and lights. Unless I have a series of six houses, that means I can't incorporate every color I love into every room I have. Or can I?

Keeping your base pieces neutral does two things. First, it makes you focus on other remarkable aspects about the pieces themselves since you're not relying on color to be the selling point and carry the style. Instead you focus on shape or silhouette or scale, or maybe the material itself. You have to up your game and create interest within the neutral palette, which to me is such a fun and rewarding limit.

But I still like color, and this is where the fun happens. You can add color in ways that you can easily change without going bankrupt. Instead of buying a new sofa every time you crave a new color, you buy a pink pillow cover, candles, or flowers. When you decide you now need greens and blues in your life, you simply move the stack of pink books back onto the bookshelf and **shop the house** (#38) for a few green and blue items.

The key to my commitment to neutral investment pieces was knowing that I could have fun with color if, where, and when I chose without getting tied up in a long-term relationship with a particular hue. What a relief. ■

84

Find your personal neutrals

MOST OF THE RULES in this book are ones I've chanted and taught and implemented in my own houses for ages. This one I discovered yesterday. As I'm writing, I'm also making decisions for a few pieces. I need to finish some rooms before I take photos.

When we moved in, the beadboard walls of a tiny room that used to be a porch were painted a pretty shade of light blue. It suited the room but wasn't a shade I loved. So I chose a go-to paint color I've used in the past, Sherwin Williams Oyster Bay, and we kept it blue but this time with a green undertone. It's a green-blue that has magically worked for me in many houses even though I major in neutral colors.

I also needed an ottoman or coffee table for the porch, and I knew I wanted something round because it's a thin room, only six feet wide, and round tables are easier to navigate around. Plus, with all the right angles happening in the windowpanes and lines of the beadboard walls, I wanted to **round it off and add curves** (#78). I was also hoping to find something upholstered. Because the room is tiny, I wanted to take every opportunity to add softness, especially since I made a purposeful decision to not hang drapes because I believe this room is better with naked windows.

I ended up finding a cushy round ottoman in the most exquisite rusty brown, and I was shocked to see it showing up with the green-blue in this house because I've used versions of both those colors in my last seven houses over the past twenty years. What? In that moment I realized that, just like we all have **timeless classics** (#23) with our furniture pieces, fabrics, patterns, and silhouettes, most of us have a few colors that we love being surrounded by.

Although all of my houses have had different **bosses I had to respect** (#20)—mostly in the way of flooring, from pinky wood to terra-cotta to orange wood to dark brown wood—I'm shocked that versions of these two colors were able to work their way in and get along with every boss. They've become so easy to use that for me they're like neutrals.

Look around your home and notice the colors you love being surrounded by. Are there any particular colors that have traveled with you and keep showing up, respecting all the bosses they come in contact with? These are your personal neutrals. ▪

For a larger photo of the room mentioned here, see House Rule 78.

HOUSE RULES IN ACTION: 3 Limitations lead to innovations
5 Resourcefulness is the ultimate resource 7 You can't ruin
something you already hate 15 It doesn't have to be perfect to
be beautiful 22 Test it before you invest in it 52 Layer your light
59 Don't gallery-wall by accident 66 If it sits out it's a decoration
68 Cluster your collections 72 Plant math 73 It doesn't have to be
living to add life 75 Surfaces declare their purposes 76 Let your
refrigerator run around naked

Change doesn't happen without changing.

Pattern fills a room

IF YOU HAVE a small room that feels a bit full or cluttered and you've already decluttered what isn't needed, removing some pattern will help quiet it down. Pattern visually fills up a space and is louder than a solid color. If a room feels like it's closing in on you or if you simply need a quick change, see if you can remove or neutralize any patterns. Switching out patterned pillows for solid, layering a smaller solid rug over a big patterned carpet, or pairing a solid throw with a busy sofa can calm, quiet, and simplify a room, instantly making it feel a little larger.

The opposite is true as well. Maybe you moved to a new place that's huge or you have a big empty room that you want to feel cozy while using less. If you have a vast space and you want it to quickly feel fuller, add a pattern in the form of wallpaper, drapes, or rugs.

The larger a pattern's scale, the louder and bossier it is. When we walk into a room where patterns are used, our eyes often go to the largest pattern first. The same is true when a pattern uses contrasting colors. Muted patterns are quieter than vibrant,

large, high-contrast patterns. Use that information wisely to draw attention to what you want others to see and let solid colors fade a bit into the background.

Texture is also a form of pattern. A heavy texture like grass cloth wallpaper, a jute rug, or slubby linen drapes can act as a monochromatic pattern. Organic materials like veiny marble or open dark wood grain, or even the louvers in wood shutters add texture and pattern to a space.

If you **quiet your room** (#36) and see what it looks like **naked** (#37), you might discover that it's already full of pattern. Does it have interesting wall treatments like beadboard or picture frame molding? Is there a tile or wood pattern happening in the floor? Does the ceiling have texture, paneling, or beams? If your room is born with pattern, you might not need to add much with your decor. If your room is a plain, smooth square box, you might have to work in more pattern to achieve the look you want.

Combining too many patterns can feel disjointed and busy, but too few can feel sterile and cold. You get to find that perfect mix for your personal style. When it comes to patterns, finding your perfect mix of scale, texture, and color is an enjoyable part of design if you know to pay attention to it. And now you do. ■

86

Remember the sabbath and keep it homey

A SABBATH is about rest and focus. I'm no theologian, so I won't try to go further than that. But I do know that purposefully setting aside time to rest allows us to have the space to focus on what matters.

It's exactly the same with our home.

You do not need to fill every empty wall with art, every surface with tchotchkes, every shelf with books. It's actually more meaningful when you don't. Think about when you go into an art gallery. Each piece is often surrounded by an expanse of negative space. The larger the negative space, the more we're drawn to the art. That's not a mistake. It's done purposefully.

In our homes, we should purposely provide negative or empty space for the eye—or eyes if you have two (interior decorating joke there)—to rest. Isn't that a lovely thought that also takes some pressure off?

My personal style lends itself to keeping lots of wall sabbaths. But I also love a series of shelves where one is kept empty, a bed with just the essentials, a homey home where enough is considered better than more. Tim Ferriss has a list of seventeen questions that changed his life. Question 11 asks, "What if I could only subtract to solve problems?"

What if you could only subtract to make changes in your home? What if what your home needs isn't more of the right stuff but less of the excess?

Consider if your space could use a wall pause, a bare chair, a bed with no spread, or a **floor with no more** (#87). ■

87

Store on the floor no more

MY MOM SAYS when the floors are clean the whole house is clean, and I sometimes hate her for it because it's so very true and floors are my nemesis. I would much rather talk about decorating than cleaning, but this idea is related to both, so when you follow it you can feel extra accomplished. Two birds and all.

When my boys were younger, we used baskets to store their toys, diaper stuff, craft stuff, library books, and a million other things. I loved how baskets helped to visually quiet the stuff of life we needed at our fingertips, so I started using baskets for everything and still love a good basket to this day. On the floor next to the sofa I placed a basket for magazines. By the back door I kept a shallow basket for shoes. I slid a basket with my nail polish under the sofa. On the stairs I placed a stairstep-shaped basket to hold upstairs things I would always forget to grab the next time I was going up the stairs. Look at me corralling all my loose ends into decorative baskets!

I'm also always on the lookout for stuff I can declutter and donate, and the experts say you should always have a donation bin by your back door where you can easily toss unwanted items. I took their advice. I also don't have a good system for recycling, so our entire family just piles boxes and recyclables next to the back door like animals. I wish this were a lie, but as I type this there is a pile of stuff by the door to donate and recycle.

This all sounds acceptable, but what it looks like in real life is full floors. Especially at our poor back door. Not only do my floors hold rugs and furniture like God intended, but they have many random items that weren't actually meant to be stored on the floor indefinitely. The result is that my house looks and feels cluttered, messy, and overwhelming.

Here's one way you can tell if you have Floor-Storing Syndrome like me. The next time you go to mop, pay attention to what you have to pick up off the floor and then put back on the floor when you're done. Once I became aware of how often I chose to store things on the floor, I began to make an effort to change that. It makes a surprising difference in the visual clutter and how tidy my house feels. Once again, Mom was right. ■

88

Collected over time

THIS IS ONE of those rules that's been passed down through generations of designers. Most of us have heard about the idea of creating a room that looks as if it is (and hopefully has been) collected over time. But why? And what in the world does that actually mean?

There have been moments in my life when I've been so fed up with a space that I wished I could go out to one store and instantly purchase all new items for the room. Just start over completely fresh and have it be done. It suddenly seems so simple to go to the nearest furniture store and buy everything as a set.

But I know better. When you purchase everything on the same day from the same place, it's highly likely that one day in the foreseeable future you will be in your space and suddenly hate everything on the same day. When you add and subtract over time, you'll always have a few things you love rotating in and out and other items that can be retired.

By combining the new sofa, the classic jute rug, the vintage side table, the art from your grandmother's home, the pottery pinch pot your youngest made in elementary school, and your husband's twenty-year-old favorite chair, you create a story with a sense of history and meaning. There is a groundedness we experience when we decorate with items that were born before us and will continue being used after we're gone.

If you do find yourself needing to purchase all new items at once, shop different stores and be sure to **disrupt the timeline** (#63) by using pieces from different eras. That will help ensure that even though you acquired pieces at the same time, they weren't created in the same time frame, which will result in a longer life. ■

Vintage cabinet paired with a ten-year-old lamp, an imperfect planter, DIY art, and new drapes.

89

Choose your trouble

ALL PROGRESS takes trouble. No one gets a free pass.

Choosing a paint color, going to the paint store, buying the paint, making small talk with the paint mixer person, pretending like you are confident on the sheen you are using, gathering all the supplies, prepping the room, answering questions your family keeps asking, taping off or painting straight lines, protecting your floors, keeping the cat out of the paint, and the actual act of painting. It's all trouble.

Calling the painter, getting the quote, communicating the exact colors and sheens, emptying the room, locking up the cat, making yourself presentable, staying home or keeping the door unlocked, having painters in and out of your house, providing bathroom access, earning the money to pay the painters, then paying them. Also trouble.

Researching sofas, scouring Facebook Marketplace for months, creating keyword alerts, looking for that dreamy vintage sofa, communicating with a vintage sofa seller who might possibly be an axe murderer, going to see the sofa, purchasing the sofa after updating your Venmo app, borrowing a truck, getting a friend's help and actually moving a sofa you found for a steal. Trouble.

Putting on people clothes and walking into a store where they sell custom sofas, answering all the salesclerk's questions, taking time to make confident decisions on fabric, color, down-wrapped cushions, depth, width, welting, fabric protection, and delivery options. Waiting for three to four months while your custom sofa is being made, earning and saving the money and paying for your custom sofa, tipping the delivery guys, finding the cat who escaped during delivery. *Trouble.*

Maybe you enjoy the hunt and stopping in at your local thrift store every week. Although it's a commitment, when it pays off you love that feeling of finding beauty in something someone else discarded.

Maybe you're skilled at researching, learning, and figuring things out. DIYing is still work, yes, but it's especially rewarding for you.

Maybe you've got some money saved up. Although there might be cheaper alternatives if you had the time or inspiration, where you are right now in life you need to pay someone else to do the job. It's such a relief to not have to think.

All good things require a form of trouble and a form of risk. And when it works out and you find your trouble sweet spot, you forget about the pain of the trouble. The good news is, most of us have the privilege of choosing our trouble. Learn to know yourself and choose wisely. ▪

90

The size of your house doesn't dictate the size of your hospitality

WHEN YOU'RE INVITED into someone's house for the first time, how are you hoping to feel?

Do you hope to be impressed, dazzled, and surrounded by vastness and perfection? Absolutely not. You would hate that person and feel like you have to self-promote, show off, and mention all the highlight reel moments of your life. Sounds exhausting.

I know you and I both know this, but we have to hear it over and over. When we invite someone over to our house, they aren't yearning to be impressed by us. No one is hoping they'll come into our house and be intimidated and awestruck by its grandeur and our personal greatness.

We want people to come into our home and have it feel relatable and comfortable. We want them to relax, feel seen, and experience connection. Our home can work with us to accomplish this goal, and not having a huge gold-plated mansion is one way to do this.

Oh, your house is tiny? Who cares. Is it welcoming? That's what counts. Most of us can easily think back to a time when someone offered up true, meaningful hospitality, and it had nothing to do with the size or state of their house.

No, if your home is 850 square feet you won't be hosting the reception for your daughter's wedding with four hundred guests. But every home has a limit in that sense. Besides, did you know a house isn't required in order to host and be hospitable? Hospitality is a mindset. You can do it at an Airbnb, a picnic area in a park, a church fellowship hall, or an intimate table at a restaurant.

Every year Chad and I take a trip with our good friends Greg and Caroline, and a few years ago one of our excursions was a chilly sunset cruise on a sailboat. In October. In Maine. There were fifty or so people on the "cruise" where grown adult volunteers pulled ropes, got splashed, and then tried to balance at a thirty-degree angle on a bench with no back while holding a glass of wine.

Greg and Chad did what they always do and began to meet our backless-bench neighbors. They asked questions and listened to the answers, told funny stories and jokes, and shared their bottle of bourbon with the people right in our vicinity. Caroline and I watched as our husbands practiced hospitality in their corner of our floating world during an unremarkable sunset. Hospitality is about creating an environment where others feel seen, heard, and cared for. No house required.

Your house might not be perfect, but your hospitality is exactly what we need. ■

91

Stop saving for someday

IN HER BOOK *Decluttering at the Speed of Life*, Dana K. White writes, "There's a difference between something being useful and actually using something." Dang, did that line burn.

If you follow decluttering and organizing experts, they talk about our fantasy selves and how, when it comes to stuff, we often hold on to things we'll never use—such as supplies for crafts and hobbies we've given up—because we save them for our future fantasy selves. Not only do we have fantasy selves, but we also have fantasy decor, fantasy homes, and fantasy circumstances. Deciphering between the useful, the used, and (dare I say) the misused can help us weed out the fantasy stuff in our homes.

Just because something is used doesn't mean it has earned the right to stay in your home. For years I kept a beautiful, well-made, yet massively huge and heavy wood armoire in our small home. It was designed for those boxy, old-timey TVs we used to have before flatscreens came out. Long ago we all hid our TVs in big chunky armoires with doors that closed, and I have to admit I kind of miss being able to close doors over the television.

Once we upgraded to a flatscreen I didn't want to get rid of our beautiful armoire. Because I'm always looking for creative possibilities, I thought it could be repurposed. What if we moved to a house without closets? It would be so easy to rebuild the inside and add a rod for hanging clothes. So until we moved to this closetless house, we kept the largest, heaviest, bulkiest piece of furniture we owned in our small bedroom and misused it as a bookshelf. It made for the world's worst bookshelf, by the way, because it was tremendously deep. And had no actual shelves. Just a big, square vastness.

Although in theory an armoire is useful, and we even found a use for it, we weren't using it well. We were only using about 10 percent of its capacity, and it took up a bunch of space and made our lives difficult in every way but one: I got to avoid making a decision. (Which—guess what?—meant I was actually making a decision to keep something that wasn't working!)

It's hard getting rid of something that has served you well in the past. But I have to remind myself that I'm not living in the past or in a fantasy, and my books deserve an actual bookshelf. ■

92

Life is a special occasion

SPECIAL THINGS aren't meant to be saved for special circumstances but enjoyed with special people.

One way we make sure that happens is to set our home up in a way that allows special and meaningful items to be used, admired, and appreciated. Pull out the good hand lotion and put it next to the bed. Chill the dusty bottle of wine. Eat pizza in the formal dining room.

Think about the things in your home that are the most special and meaningful. Are they being enjoyed? It's worth it to make sure they are. Maybe you need to display the christening gown on a beautiful hanger on the wall, open the photo album to your favorite page and show it off in the front entry, or frame the artwork in an over-the-top gilded frame and look at it every morning.

If life truly is a special occasion, then let's treat it that way.

Light that candle.

Wear the perfume.

Fill the bath with the fancy stuff.

Buy the 30-foot-tall inflatable snowman.

Eat spaghetti on the good dishes.

Tear the tags off that dress and wear it with tennis shoes.

Cut all the lilacs and make a bouquet.

Make the nail holes and hang those pictures.

Plant the dreamy bulbs even if you aren't sure they'll bloom.

Find a place to use your favorite wallpaper.

Highlight the best parts of the high-end coffee table book.

Paint stripes on the wall.

Enlarge the photo and have it framed.

Display the trophy.

Get a cat.

Buy the useless chaise lounge.

Pick the cool one.

Use the weird one.

Honor your own style.

We have got to stop waiting and start enjoying our special things because someday is now. ▪

93

Add a spoonful of sugar

JAMES CLEAR SAYS, "Environment is the invisible hand that shapes human behavior." It's one of my personal mottos because, on the very rare occurrence when I feel like I'm wasting my life talking about pillow covers and lamp bases, it reminds me that no, this is not a waste. Creating an environment on purpose is powerful. And the environment we spend the most time in is our home. It's a reminder of the truth we already know: our surroundings deeply affect our mood, actions, thoughts, and feelings.

One of the most important things I want to be sure to include in my home is a sense of joy. The most obvious way to add joy to a home is by having a joyful attitude, but that's not what this book is about. How can we add a visual representation of joy to our homes? By adding in a dash of playfulness and lightheartedness and not taking things too seriously. It creates a sense of the unexpected in a memorable way.

When we add the unexpected, often we are purposely breaking some sort of decorating rule to grab attention in a good way. Not because we don't know better but because it makes the room better. Now that you know about **nailing that scale** (#39), you can break that rule to such an extreme that it creates a sense of joy for those who notice. **Learn the rules to break the rules** (#1), remember?

Purposely adding in something tiny—like a teeny ceramic animal tucked into the moss of a potted plant or a miniature piece of art hung in an unexpected place—surprises, delights, and rewards the one who pays attention.

The opposite is true too. Adding an oversized piece like a giant faceted gold gem table announces to everyone that you don't take yourself or your home too seriously.

In her book *Joyful*, Ingrid Fetell Lee suggests that certain shapes like circles, dots, and spheres can add a sense of play. Wide stripes evoke a circus tent that naturally feels jovial and laid-back. After reading Ingrid's book I looked for more ways to add circles and wide stripes to our home.

You can create a sense of cheer by grouping traditional items in a nontraditional way, by color blocking with an unexpected color, and even by incorporating **rainbowetical order** (#77). The more fancy and sophisticated your house, the more whimsy you can add without it feeling unbalanced or overly childish. ■

94

Find your taxidermy

MY FRIEND KENDRA visited our new-to-us home for the first time and remarked that seeing our vintage stuffed fox, pheasant, and pronghorn along with rabbit pelts and antlers around the house made her momentarily question if she should add some taxidermy to her own home. She quickly realized that wasn't the reason she liked our house and that it was the layers, the coziness, and the functionality that made her feel welcome. But the "dead animals," as she pointed out, also added a sense of life and texture, and that's what she noticed first. Then she declared she was going to find her own version of taxidermy. I declared her brilliant and decided that needed to be a house rule. So here we are.

I believe the uniquely personal sense of self that taxidermy adds to our home is the cherry on top. When it comes down to it, it's just weird and unexpected and works. "Keep Austin Weird" has got to be the best slogan in Texas and possibly the world. And I believe we should apply that to our homes too. Let's make home weird again!

We should define *weird* because, well, if we don't it could get ugly—literally. But maybe that's part of the fun. Adding a sense of weirdness is sort of like adding the signature pieces to your home. You know when a person gives you that not-quite-but-almost compliment of "Oh, I love that for you," pointing out something that's good for you but maybe not for them? Let's apply that to decorating and make it a goal to add something weird or just a tiny bit quirky.

If that scares you, great. Make it tiny, sneak it in. I like to think that we all have weird stuff hiding somewhere and we should embrace it. What do you love? What are you obsessed with? What do you want to be surrounded by? Pull it out of storage and put it on a shelf.

It might be weird, odd, or a crazy curiosity, or it might simply be meaningful to you in a way that no one else needs to know. Every house should reflect the people who live there in its own unique way, and every space deserves to be weird if it wants.

Do what Kendra suggested: go find your own version of taxidermy and display it proudly. ■

Make it awe-full

DECORATORS WILL PREACH about bringing the outside in, and rightly so. We should all strive to have a bit of nature indoors. I'm a fan of **adding life, even if it's not living** (#73). But I like to take it a step further and surround myself with not just something from the natural world but something that creates a sense of awe.

Something that inspires awe—be it a vista, a work of art, or an object from creation—has a way of putting us in our place in a good way. I love to include awe-full items in our home to remind us of the beauty of the natural world and our place within it.

I **found my literal taxidermy** (#94), but you don't have to use taxidermy to include some awe. Maybe you took a gorgeous photo of a sunset. Have it printed and framed! Maybe you have a beautiful blooming tree outside your window. Open the drapes! Maybe you simply turn on YouTube to a snowy landscape or beach scene and enjoy it in the background.

I'm currently loving my crystal tea light candleholders with their haphazard offshoots of opaque white rock. They are otherworldly. I love how certain facets catch the light and sparkle, but they are still raw and imperfect with broken pieces and parts that look like they weren't finished growing. Those crystals, which obviously were not mass-produced, have a quiet ability of putting me in my place in this world in a way that I like.

Keep your eyes open for something awe-inspiring to include in your home and be reminded of the beauty of the earth. ■

96

Home is a feeling

IT'S BEEN SAID that home is a feeling, and I would agree. But what does that actually mean, and how in the world do we capture that feeling? Is it possible to create that feeling on purpose? I say yes, and it's simple if you understand how.

We experience our world and develop a sense of place through our five senses: what we smell, hear, taste, touch, and see. That's all we get to use to create the aesthetic of home.

It's 6:59 on a February morning, just now getting light out, and I'm currently sitting in a cushy chair with my computer on my lap. I'm just a few feet from the fireplace where a cozy fire flickers. I've got a reading light perched low over my chair, creating the perfect puddle of warm light right where I need it. My iced coffee is sitting within reach, and I can smell a mix of the coconut lotion I put on this morning along with the lingering scent of the jasmine plant that I bought from the grocery store last week and have yet to kill. The fire isn't one we built from logs all popping and crackling, but even a gas fireplace turned on with a switch creates background noise. The dog sighs heavily, and Chad turns the pages of his book where he sits across from me. This feels like home.

We get to control so many aspects of how we experience home, and only part of this is visual. It doesn't matter where we are geographically or whether we are living in our dream house. Creating an environment of home isn't about high-end choices and keeping up with trends. It's not about pursuing one particular style. It's about creating an atmosphere where we feel seen, loved, and heard.

You create the look of home by purposely choosing functional and meaningful beauty.

You create the sounds of home by paying attention to the background noises and providing a soundtrack to your life in the wind chimes you hang, the words you speak, the literal playlists you keep on repeat through your speakers.

You create the feel of home by the temperature, the throws, the materials, the objects you come in physical contact with as you move through your house.

You create the scent of home with flowers cut from the yard, favorite scents you bring in, perfume you wear, and soaps you use.

You create the taste of home by providing food and drink. It doesn't have to be fancy, but it all leads to the complete experience of *home*. ■

97

Risk—take some and pass it on

NOT ALL RISKS are created equal. Choosing a finish on a photo frame isn't as risky as choosing a fabric for a custom sofa isn't as risky as moving across the country to a place you've never been and starting a new job. The good news is, home is the ideal place to practice risk-taking!

The best way to learn how to make better decisions in your home is to start making decisions even when your circumstances aren't perfect, because your **resourcefulness is your greatest resource** (#5). You'll either make a great decision or you'll get to evaluate your mistakes and learn how to make a better decision next time. It's a free design school if you pay attention.

After decorating fifteen of my own houses, writing four design books, and teaching thousands of women how to make better decorating decisions, I still second-guess myself. I'm rarely fully confident that something will for sure turn out. But over the years I've learned more about my personal style, my **timeless classics** (#23), and what works for me. I've paid attention to what I hate and tried to figure out why I don't like something. I **baby-stepped my way** (#6) and risked up as my confidence grew.

If your confidence is quivering, here's a little practice that enables you to learn from decisions you've already made. Ask yourself a few questions to help minimize risk in your home:

- What have you changed in your home that you love, and what do you love about it?
- What have you changed that you're not thrilled with? Why?
- What was the best money you spent on your home?
- What projects were worth your time and energy?
- What projects didn't pan out? Why not?

Asking questions like this helped me create a few of **my own house rules** (#98). Once I realized I was always unhappy with large colorful pieces, I made it a point to invest in more neutrals. When I realized I always ended up hating store-bought paintings, I decided **I couldn't ruin something I already hated** (#7) and painted over the canvases.

Making decisions in your home is the only way to make decorating progress. A less-than-perfect decision becomes a normal part of life that doesn't have to be feared when you allow yourself to learn from it and decide to keep moving forward anyway. Not only is this great practice for all aspects of life, but it's also a wonderful attitude to pass on to your children, friends, and family. Let them see you taking calculated risks and learning from them. The world needs better risk-takers, change-makers, and I-wonder-ifers, because change isn't possible without changing. ■

98

Make your own house rules

BECOME A STUDENT of yourself. We all have personal preferences, pet peeves, likes and dislikes. No matter what the trends or gurus say, we've got our **splurges and don't-cares** (#29).

It's taken me years—YEARS—to learn one of my own private and personal decorating truths that *only* applies to me and is not for you. Here it is:

I want my **life full** of color and my home **full** of **neutrals.**

For years I've been secretly at war with myself. I've felt like if I don't embrace using bold colors in my home, then it must mean I'm afraid of them or don't know what I'm doing or not risky or not on trend or just flat-out boring. And maybe that's all true. All I know is that every time I've taken a risk and added a bold color, within a year or two all I can think about is how to neutralize that color because it's become my master.

For me, bold color on large pieces takes away my freedom and bosses my attention and hems me into one particular look and scheme for way too long. And without fail I always, ALWAYS end up changing it.

Even though I love and crave color, *for me* using loud color on large investment pieces is using color incorrectly.

A few years ago, before I declared this rule to myself, we upgraded to a king-size bed. I found a beautiful wingback velvet bed in the most luscious emerald green. I was heartbroken to discover that color was backordered for months. So I ended up ordering the same bed in black, and not a day goes by when I don't thank baby Jesus, my lucky stars, and every coin I've ever thrown into a fountain that the green bed wasn't an option.

I would have felt imprisoned by that bed in a matter of weeks, I just know it. That bed would have never worked three years later when we moved to our next house. Plus, I would have gotten tired of being forced to incorporate a particular shade of bossy green for the life of the bed. Crisis averted. Now I have my own rule that I've learned to obey so I'm not tempted.

The walls in our room are painted in one of my **personal neutrals** (#84), and when I want a splash of color, I add some pretty pillows and a throw, flowers, books, and accessories, not some expensive piece of furniture I'll need to use for years. **I commit to low-commitment color** (#83).

I'm SO glad I'm not married to a green bed.

As for me and my house, I'll keep the big stuff neutral. ■

99

Make a "We Did It" List

YEARS AGO, when we had a huge ugly amount of debt to pay off, sometimes the only thing that gave me hope was to add up the amount we had already paid off, circling and highlighting that number, announcing it to Chad, and comparing it to the last time I added it all up. Every single time, without fail, I was surprised and motivated to keep going.

You are doing this. You are making meaningful changes in your home. You're learning from your mistakes. You're understanding yourself and how to make better decorating decisions. You're creating a home that serves your family. It's worth the trouble.

Here's what to do if and when you get discouraged. Grab a sheet of paper and write "We Did It!" at the top. Then simply start writing out every single thing you can think of that made a difference in your home in the past whenever since you moved there.

Pressure washed the porch? Write it down. Water heater died and you had to buy a new one? On the list. Maybe you moved your sofa to accommodate an extra chair for more seating. That counts too!

I want you to give yourself as much credit as possible for all the big and little, visible and invisible things you accomplished that made your home life better.

Get up and walk through each room and go outside so you don't miss anything. Look back through photos to help jog your memory. Nothing is too small for the We Did It List.

Here are some things from my past We Did It Lists:

- Put new swivel hardware on my office chairs.
- Organized the spice drawer.
- Planted three more clematis vines around the house.
- Moved the top of the hutch to the other side of the kitchen. (I had wanted to do this for a year, but it's SO heavy and I wasn't sure I'd like it. Update: I like it!)
- Changed out the side door hardware.
- Hung a new chandelier over the table.

First reflecting on what you've accomplished is the best way to move forward and think about what you hope to do in the future. Chad and I kick off our goal setting for the new year by reviewing what we did in the previous year.

Nothing is more motivating and satisfying than looking back at what you've done and remembering that it's worth it to create a life-giving home.

Make your own We Did It List, and I bet you'll be shocked at all you've accomplished. ■

100

There is no done

I TITLED THIS last section "Finish What You Started," and I have the nerve to end it by telling you that there is no such thing as done.

I hope that's endlessly freeing, because being in-process means there's room for improvement.

Decorating isn't easy, but it can be enjoyable and rewarding. Why would we want that to end?

Home could be done if people never changed. But we change our minds and change our jobs. Kids grow up. Parents get older. We pick up new hobbies and drop old ones. Home is ever evolving, and that is a wonderful thing. Part of creating home is being attuned to those changes and adjusting appropriately in the most beautiful way that serves the needs you have.

You are so good at this. Half of design is simply paying attention, and most people never even get that far. You are making a difference just by creating home with purpose that enhances the lives of those who enter.

As you move forward, I hope you continue to do what you know, find ways to use what you have, and finish the great work you've started. Here's to home. ■

100 HOUSE RULES

1 Learn the rules to break the rules 13, 123, 217
2 Find a mindset you can model 14, 50
3 Limitations lead to innovations 17, 53, 78, 137, 193, 196
4 Home exists to serve people, not the other way around 18, 177
5 Resourcefulness is the ultimate resource 21, 77, 196–97, 225
6 Baby-step your way 22, 130, 142, 169, 178, 225
7 You can't ruin something you already hate 22, 25, 69, 122–23, 196–97, 225
8 One sane space 26, 29
9 Start at the heart and work your way out 29
10 Minimal is a form of enough 30
11 Luxury isn't having more, it's needing less 33, 38
12 Admire, don't acquire 34
13 Cozy doesn't mean cluttered 37
14 Having it all is a lot to keep clean 38
15 It doesn't have to be perfect to be beautiful 41, 46–47, 123, 196
16 Be your own house whisperer 42
17 Inspiration leads to motivation 42, 45
18 Clarity creates confidence 50, 74
19 Every home has a silver lining 53
20 Respect your boss 17, 50, 46–47, 54, 93, 109, 123, 194
21 Style is found in the combinations 57, 110, 146, 149
22 Test it before you invest in it 58, 94, 196
23 Find your own timeless classics 61, 82, 123, 194, 225
24 Ignore the builder 62
25 Plan on the kids growing up 65
26 What's the third way? 66, 69
27 Add a temporary fix to the mix 66, 69
28 Amateur guesstimate or professional estimate? 70
29 Know your splurges and don't-cares 46–47, 73, 226
30 Ask why 74
31 Other ways to pay 21, 73, 77
32 It doesn't have to be symmetrical to be balanced 46–47, 78, 122–23, 133
33 Just because something costs less doesn't mean you're saving money 81, 165
34 Timelessness is here to stay 81, 82
35 Let it be easy 85, 133, 137
36 Quiet the house 90, 93, 201
37 Does your room look good naked? 93, 201
38 Shop the house 94, 126, 141, 193
39 Nail that scale 78, 97, 114, 129, 141, 142, 165, 217
40 Hate the sofa, hate the space 98
41 Pair famous couples in design 46–47, 101, 130, 133
42 Use skirts and show some leg 102
43 Count every chair and prioritize tushies 46–47, 73, 105, 106, 133
44 Incognito seato 105, 106, 122–23
45 How big is your chest? 109
46 Marry mismatched furniture and divorce the sets 110
47 Paint later 113
48 Trust the homey trinity 114

49 The floor is lava 46–47, 114, 117
50 Drapes cover the wall, not the window 114, 118, 121
51 Don't start your art until your drapes are hung correctly 121
52 Layer your light 46, 114, 126, 196
53 Let your light speak 129
54 Pick the one that scares you 130
55 Friends, not twins 122–23, 132, 133
56 Twins, not friends 46–47, 133
57 When in doubt, carry it out 85, 137, 153
58 The art of the mirror is what it reflects 138
59 Don't gallery-wall by accident 141, 196–97
60 Try the low-commitment lean 142
61 Depart from sad art 145
62 Combine the opposites 17, 97, 129, 130, 146, 149
63 Disrupt the timeline 149, 206
64 Contrast is queen if you want to be seen 18, 46, 122–23, 150
65 Subtle but significant 153
66 If it sits out, it's a decoration 129, 154, 161, 174, 181, 196
67 Stored away or on display 161, 162
68 Cluster your collections 162, 181, 196
69 The rule of pineapple 165
70 Layers invite 166
71 Get your greens 46–47, 169, 185
72 Plant math 169, 170, 196
73 It doesn't have to be living to add life 173, 196, 221
74 Aim for home base 46, 173, 174
75 Surfaces declare their purposes 177, 196
76 Let your refrigerator run around naked 178, 196
77 Rainbowetical order 181, 217
78 Round it off and add curves 122–23, 182, 194
79 Vase your space 185
80 Threes, please 186
81 Use repoofable pillows 122–23, 189
82 Trendy or trending 190
83 Commit to low-commitment color 193, 226
84 Find your personal neutrals 194, 226
85 Pattern fills a room 201
86 Remember the sabbath and keep it homey 122–23, 202
87 Store on the floor no more 202, 205
88 Collected over time 149, 206
89 Choose your trouble 93, 209
90 The size of your house doesn't dictate the size of your hospitality 123, 210
91 Stop saving for someday 213
92 Life is a special occasion 214
93 Add a spoonful of sugar 46, 217
94 Find your taxidermy 218, 221
95 Make it awe-full 221
96 Home is a feeling 222
97 Risk—take some and pass it on 225
98 Make your own house rules 193, 225, 226
99 Make a "We Did It" List 229
100 There is no done 230

ACKNOWLEDGMENTS

SPECIAL THANKS to the Cozy Minimalist Community who workshopped the idea of writing down all these quirky rules with me from the beginning. Extra special thanks to community member Tami Vik who suggested the name House Rules. As soon as you mentioned it, we all knew it was right.

Unending thanks go out to:

Emily and John Freeman

Caroline and Greg TeSelle

Tim and Chris Willard

Caleb and Ana Peavy and the Unmutable team, especially Jessica, Josh, and Kam

Karen and Curtis Yates and the entire Yates & Yates team

Karrie Dobie, Megan Mazzucco, and Ginna Neel

Jerome Daley

Kendra Adachi

Jeanne Oliver

The team at Revell and Baker Publishing, including but not limited to Kelsey Bowen, William Overbeeke, Amy Nemecek, Eileen Hanson, Kelli Smith, Brianna DeWitt, and Laura Klynstra

Our couple friends, who I just realized all have last names that start with W: the Whittles, the Walls, and the Wolframs

The Depot at Gibson Mill in Concord, The Screen Door in Asheville, Main St. Antiques & Design Gallery in Mooresville, Sleepy Poet Antique Mall in Charlotte, and Thistle & Twig in Morganton

Dr. and Mrs. Plyler

Family in North Carolina, Indiana, and Wisconsin

The town of Morganton

Landis, Cademon, and Gavin

Chad, I'm so glad you said it was time to move. Let's buy another old house! ■

NOTES

85 **In his book Effortless:** Greg McKeown, *Effortless: Make It Easier to Do What Matters Most* (New York: Currency, 2021).

109 **Dana K. White, an organizing and decluttering expert:** For more on the Container Concept, see Dana K. White, "Containers and Limits and How They'll Change Your Life!," episode 7 of *A Slob Comes Clean* (podcast), October 11, 2013, https://www.aslobcomes clean.com/2013/10/007-containers-and-limits-and-how-theyll-change-your-life/.

166 **In his book The Beauty Chasers:** Timothy D. Willard, *The Beauty Chasers: Recapturing the Wonder of the Divine,* (Grand Rapids: Zondervan, 2022), 143–44.

170 **"Pick what you like, then see how it grows":** Emily P. Freeman, *The Next Right Thing: A Simple, Soulful Practice for Making Life Decisions* (Grand Rapids: Revell, 2019), 201.

202 **"What if I could only subtract to solve problems?":** Tim Ferriss, "17 Questions That Changed My Life," accessed June 22, 2023, https://tim.blog/wp-content/uploads/2020 /01/17-Questions-That-Changed-My-Life.pdf.

213 **"There's a difference between something being useful and actually using something":** Dana K. White, *Decluttering at the Speed of Life: Winning Your Never-Ending Battle with Stuff* (Nashville: Thomas Nelson, 2018), 51.

217 **"Environment is the invisible hand that shapes human behavior":** James Clear, *Atomic Habits: An Easy and Proven Way to Build Good Habits and Break Bad Ones* (New York: Avery, 2018), 82.

217 **In her book Joyful:** Ingrid Fetell Lee, *Joyful: The Art of Finding Happiness All Around You* (New York: Little, Brown Spark, 2018), 8.

MYQUILLYN SMITH, also known as "The Nester," is the *New York Times* and *Wall Street Journal* bestselling author of *Welcome Home* and *Cozy Minimalist Home*. For the past seventeen years, she has been encouraging women to embrace their space—imperfections and all—and make it their own. Her home in North Carolina has been featured in *Better Homes & Gardens*, *Ladies' Home Journal*, and *Cottages & Bungalows*. She's never met a home she didn't love.

CONNECT WITH MYQUILLYN

TheNester.com

AcademyOfHome.com

 @thenester

 Want to experience more House Rules in action?
Scan the QR code or go to TheNester.com/HouseRules
for a video tour of Myquillyn's home.

© 2024 by Myquillyn Smith

Published by Revell
a division of Baker Publishing Group
Grand Rapids, Michigan
www.revellbooks.com

Printed in China

Library of Congress Cataloging-in-Publication Data
Names: Smith, Myquillyn, author.
Title: House rules : how to decorate for every home, style, and budget / Myquillyn Smith.
Description: Grand Rapids, Michigan : Revell, a division of Baker Publishing Group, [2024] |
    Includes bibliographical references.
Identifiers: LCCN 2023022653 | ISBN 9780800744748 (cloth) | ISBN 9781493444861 (ebook)
Subjects: LCSH: Interior decoration.
Classification: LCC NK2115 .S585 2024 | DDC 747—dc23/eng/20230605
LC record available at https://lccn.loc.gov/2023022653

Photography: Myquillyn Smith
Interior design: William Overbeeke

Published in association with Yates & Yates, www.yates2.com

Baker Publishing Group publications use paper produced from sustainable forestry practices and post-consumer waste whenever possible.

24 25 26 27 28 29 30   7 6 5 4 3 2 1